What
Would
Buddha
Do?

What Would Buddha Do?

Answers to Life's Daily Dilemmas

FRANZ METCALF, PH.D.

GRAMERCY BOOKS
NEW YORK

Quotes on pages 25, 86 and 106 originally appeared in *Kindness, Clarity,* and *Insight* by The Fourteenth Dalai Lama (pages 39, 36 and 14, respectively), Snow Lion Publications, Ithaca, NY: 1984

Quotes on pages 102 and 122 originally appeared in *The Joy of Living and Dying in Peace (Library of Tibet Series)* by the Fourteenth Dalai Lama (pages 96 and 169, respectively), Harper San Francisco, San Francisco, CA: 1997. We thank The Library of Tibet and John Avedon for permission to reprint these.

This 2002 edition is published by Gramercy Books, an imprint of Random House Value Publishing, a division of Random House, Inc., New York, by arrangement with Ulysses Press, Berkeley, California.

Gramercy is a registered trademark and the colophon is a trademark of Random House, Inc.

Random House
New York • Toronto • London • Sydney • Auckland
www.randomhouse.com

Printed in the United States of America

Interior design: Leslie Henriques, Sarah Levin

Library of Congress Cataloging-in-Publication Data

Metcalf, Franz Aubrey.
    What would Buddha do?:101 answers to life's daily dilemmas / Franz Metcalf; editor, Ray Riegert.
        p. cm.
    Originally published: v Berkeley, Calif. : Seastone, c1999.
    ISBN 0-517-22007-5
        1. Religious life—Buddhism. I. Riegert, Ray. II. Title.

BQ5405 .M48 2002
294.3'444—dc21

                                                                    2002072077

9 8 7 6 5 4 3 2

As I hope you'll see in reading it,
    I dedicate this book to the Buddhas within,
        yearning for us to give them birth.
            Namo tassa bhagavato arahato sammasambuddhassa.

Acknowledgments

I've often wondered why authors always have acknowledgment pages. They're not really for the general reader, since reading them is like going to a party where you don't know anyone. I now know the point of these pages: We all build up friendly debts in life, but we don't always have the pleasure of paying them back directly. In acknowledgments we do, and it is a great pleasure. Welcome to the party.

For this book, without qualification and from its birth, I thank Leslie Henriques, Ray Riegert and Bryce Willett for their innumerable gifts and labors, and Phil Abrams for being born. For their work, especially in the last, hectic weeks, I thank Claire Chun, Heather McCann, Steven Schwartz and the whole charming staff at Ulysses Press.

This is not an academic book, so I had better not incriminate any scholars here, but Buddha knows what they've done to guide me. I do thank Daniel Capper for his advice on Tibetan texts. Dan led me to the Dalai Lama's book, *Kindness, Clarity, and Insight*, and I thank Snow Lion Press for allowing me to quote from it here.

First and last, for me there is always Nina. First to encourage me, last to make edits, always my bunkie Buddha.

Table of Contents

Introduction	1
What's Wrong With Me?!	7
Toward a New Me	21
Pure Love	37
Lust for Life	53
Doing the Right Thing	67
Walking the Walk on the Noble Path	81
The Buddha in the Machine	97
The Big Questions	111
Suggestions for Further Reading	129

Introduction

What would Buddha do? He was, after all, a person like us. He struggled with life just as we do, and he discovered life's deepest secrets. What better role model could we desire? Picture yourself facing a personal conflict or moral dilemma; ask yourself, what would Buddha do if he were in my shoes?

"What would Buddha do?" is a great question, helpful and reassuring. But how do we answer this question—not only once, but in the trials of life? The endless richness of the Buddhist tradition provides so many answers, so many models—how do we locate them and choose those that might help?

This question, "What would Buddha do?" has recently been made more powerful by the "What Would Jesus Do?" phenomenon, a nationwide movement that encourages individuals, when facing a personal conflict or moral dilemma, to ask themselves, "What would Jesus do?" It's a powerful question, one that can change lives.

To ask such a question is to give yourself the moment of reflection it takes to find an answer. Buddhists have been doing this for 2500 years. In discovering what Buddha would do, they have plumbed a deep reservoir of practices, texts, rituals and myths.

I have drawn from this same well of Buddhist wisdom to answer the central question of what Buddha would do when faced with the many trials of our contemporary life. This book looks to the whole current of Buddhist tradition for that help, from the earliest stories of Buddha's life to the insights of awakened masters who continue the tradition today.

Who is Buddha? or, Who are You?

The historical Buddha, who lived in what is now Nepal and India, was a real person—a man who overcame desire, hatred and ignorance. Buddhism, the religion that follows his teaching, has looked back to him as an exalted teacher, even a perfected man, but never as a god. Whatever fantastic powers have been attributed to Buddha, he remains human.

Buddha was a psychologist, and called himself a doctor more than once. During his long teaching career he dispensed the medicine of insight—insight into our human problems and how to transcend them. He broke down the distinction between psychologist and religious teacher. And he created a system of thought—the Buddhist tradition—that provides very helpful and surprisingly contemporary answers to the questions each of us faces today.

Though Buddha was a historical figure, this does not exhaust the many meanings of his name. The word has come to signify not just the historical Buddha, but awakening itself, the Buddha Mind. This Buddha Mind is at once transcendent and within each of us at every moment. Just as Buddha pervades the universe, so Buddha Nature pervades us as well, making each of us, in a sense, a Buddha.

If we are Buddhas already, what is it we have to learn? Why do we still feel frustrated and disappointed? Perhaps this is because we haven't yet realized we are Buddhas. We won't realize this by indulging ourselves; we need to follow the Buddhist path leading away from the self. When we stop guiding our lives by the desires of the self, we will quite naturally live as the Buddhas we already are.

So easy to imagine, so hard to accomplish! But we've all had moments of awakening when we lived not for ourselves, not in ourselves, but in a wider, deeper flow of being. This is our real nature coming out, breaking through the crust of ego and consciousness we have layered upon it over the long days of our lives. We can all be Buddhas—we *are* all Buddhas—when we act as Buddha.

What's in this Book

This book aims to help you be the Buddha you are, to find your own Buddha Nature and allow that Nature to guide you through life. The Buddha *in you* is your best teacher. Hopefully, the questions and answers here will help you bring that Buddha to life.

The book's structure is simple: it asks 101 questions we face in living our lives. Every question is answered by Buddha—in words found in the sacred texts of Buddhism—and by a contemporary explanation of how to apply this teaching to our own lives.

Will applying these lessons really work for you personally? I think so. It's worked for me, and I am not a card-carrying Buddhist. Though

I teach Buddhism at a college, I don't belong to any Buddhist organizations and I don't chant or meditate every day. But I love Buddhism, its wisdom, and the ways it helps me be a better person. I have found that Buddha and the whole Buddhist tradition speak directly to me without demanding that I give up my freedom.

This book encourages you in your freedom. Don't just read it—use it in your own way. Whether you read it slowly for insight or turn to it under stress for advice, I hope you feel free to make it your own. Buddha asked his followers to test his words. I invite you to test these.

What's Wrong with Me?!

Tough title, I know, but we don't become better people by congratulating ourselves on our good points. Would you be reading this book if you were content to let yourself simply stay the way you were? As Buddha might tell you, you've got to keep changing. Even the deepest pool stagnates without action.

This section of the book concentrates on our typical human faults. But thankfully, Buddha does not merely chronicle our many failings, he lays out their origins and gives us clues for their eradication. I mean that literally: "eradication" means pulling up roots. Our faults are like weeds—if we really want to get rid of them we can't just take off their tops, we have to rip them out by their very roots. Taking out the root of suffering: this is what Buddha strove to embody and teach.

Each of you reading this book should find at least a couple of these questions and problems that cut right to the quick. Those are the ones you need to read again, to take to heart, to live with. What's wrong with you then becomes your spiritual path. Your anger, boredom, frustration—these become your teachers.

What would Buddha do if someone hates him?

Not by hate is hate defeated; hate is quenched by love. This is the eternal law.

Dhammapada 5

In these few words Buddha teaches what might be the greatest spiritual law. The Roman poet Virgil wrote "love conquers all." I believe there are things love is not well-suited to conquer, but love is perfectly suited to conquer hate. Why? Because it is so hard for hate to combat. Violence, revenge, sometimes even civil disobedience, add to the tremendous energy embodied in hatred. Love, on the other hand, takes the energy of hate and redirects it, as a martial artist might—only here the arts are not of war but of love. As the song tells us, "Only love can conquer hate."

Love confronts hate in the one way hate cannot comprehend, with something beyond itself—with compassion. Hate cannot go beyond itself. It draws its strength from the self's defense of self. Love lives to go beyond itself, drawing its strength from that very act. Love can thus comprehend hate, integrating it into something larger. Slowly hate is defeated, as a grain of salt dissolves into the sweetness of a pond.

What would Buddha do when a friend lets him down?

> *One should not pry into the faults of others, what they've done and left undone. Consider instead what you yourself have done and left undone.*

> **Dhammapada 50**

Buddha was sure right about this. How do I know? As country singer Hank Williams used to say, we better not mind other people's business, 'cause it's all we can do just to mind our own. Hey, when you get Buddha and Hank agreeing on something, well, it just *has* to be true. Anyway, I believe I'm safe in saying we can all testify to the truth of this advice. Living mindfully is not easy; it requires constant attention—that's the whole point. It's all we can do. Dwelling on others' failures just messes us up.

This doesn't mean we should ignore evil when we encounter it. Remember, we are all in this together: Buddha taught that we're not separate selves at all. So we should take responsibility for evil, not by decrying the deeds of others, but by overcoming them with better ones of our own. To do that we need to pay attention, especially when our deeds are not so pretty.

What would Buddha do when he gets sick?

> *He should see the body as marked by impermanence,*
> *suffering, emptiness, and lack of self. This is wisdom.*
> *But despite his broken body, he should remain in this*
> *world of birth and death, bringing benefit to all beings,*
> *never surrendering to weariness or disgust.*

Vimalakirti Sutra 5

Of course "he" in this passage is the bodhisattva, the wisdom-being we all should strive to embody. But what if that body is ailing? Yes, even Buddhas get blisters. When we face such troubles, or troubles much greater, we confront the basic lesson of life: all we see, all we touch, even our very selves are, in the end, ephemeral. Our bodies are never perfect, never free of disease, and though they stand faithful for so long, they will betray us in the end. We should treat our illness as part of life, part of our bodies.

We should not give in to disease—of course not. We should battle it for the sake of this world. But the sutra teaches us not to exhaust ourselves with avoiding all disease. We are obsessed with health in the West: we seem to think we're entitled to it. We're not. Some people drain all the life from their years in order to postpone their deaths. They may live longer, but why? In the end they too will pass away.

What would Buddha do about dieting?

> *Buddha, having emaciated himself for no reason in cruel self-abuse, realized...that this was not the way to peace, or knowledge, or liberation....One who ruins her body can never gain awakening.*

> **Buddhacharita 12.97-99**

It may seem odd to compare the two, but Buddha's striving for awakening and the modern-day compulsion to fit in that leads people to starve themselves in the name of beauty are not so far apart. Before becoming awakened, Buddha spent six years starving himself, trying to fit in with the other renunciants and break away from the impurities—the grossness—of his body. Finally after all those years he realized his self-punishment was only making him weak and confused. Remember, this was Buddha! Imagine how confused a modern teenager or dieter might be.

Let's acknowledge that self-abuse takes enormous discipline and strength and see it as a measure of our greatness of spirit. Then let's remind ourselves and our loved ones that this is the wrong way to express such greatness. Buddha was awakened soon after he began again to eat and to love his body. We must embrace and support our bodies, with all their faults; then with that renewed strength we can embrace and support each other.

What would Buddha do about lying?

In certain cases a bodhisattva may kill, steal, commit adultery, or take drugs, but he may not lie. Intentional lying contradicts reality.

Jatakas 431

It is hard to imagine Buddha killing, stealing, having sex or doing drugs. Still, given highly unusual circumstances, there are stories of Buddha doing these things, at least during his many lives as a bodhisattva, before he became fully Buddha. Of course he always did these things with the intention of saving others from ignorance and death.

In contrast, it is impossible for Buddha to lie. Buddha cannot lie, even if lying would seem to help others. Why? Because he is too in touch with reality. Lies contradict reality and blind people to the truth. Even when they help in the short run, they harm in the long run. A bodhisattva cannot do this and neither should we. Stay the course; remember, though truth may be hard at first, it is easier in the long run. As Mark Twain said, "It is easier to tell the truth: you don't have to remember anything."

What would Buddha do when facing a crisis?

> *Throw away your pitiful apathy and act boldly in this crisis! A wise person shows energy and resolve; success is in her power, no matter what.*

> **Jatakamala 14.11**

Wake up! shouts Buddha. You have the power to act, and the responsibility. The wise person shows her resolve to do her best in any circumstance. Buddha spoke these words in the teeth of a terrible storm that threatened the lives of everyone aboard his ship. Despite the danger and the need for action, the crew was apathetic. Why was this? It seems absurd.

It may be absurd to become passive in the face of danger, but it often happens, and for a variety of reasons. We doubt ourselves. We don't trust our crew. We give up hope. This is a natural tendency, and some of us live our entire lives this way. How sad, because what is the worst that can happen? Failure through inaction—that is the worst. Buddha encourages us to awaken to reality and to act. That in itself is success.

What would Buddha do when feeling frustrated?

Don't be so inconsiderate and loudly drag the furniture around the room. Likewise don't go rudely yanking doors. Find your pleasure in your deference.

Bodhicharyavatara 5.72

When frustrated, I become rude. I'm too cunning to be nasty to humans, but boy do I take it out on long-suffering objects! When I get this way I'm likely to knock something over or piss someone off and this just makes things worse. Does this remind you of anyone?

We need to heed this Buddha wisdom. It is good to direct our frustration away from people, but this is not enough. People will still feel it and can even be injured by it (driving angry is as bad as driving drunk). Instead, we have to stop the feelings of frustration. We need to question our impatience, get to its root. Why are we putting ourselves first, right now? Do we have a genuine need to take the first place? Usually, the answer is no. If the frustration remains but we overcome it, we can then give ourselves credit for our deference.

What would Buddha do about road rage?

Those who can control their rising anger as a driver controls a vehicle, those are good drivers; others only hold the reins.

Dhammapada 222

Anger afflicts us now, perhaps even more than at the time of Buddha. In the privacy of our cars we unleash our rage. We have reasons for this, and we feel safe there, but we must remember our cars are huge and deadly weapons, and other people's cars are weapons aimed at us.

Look again at what Buddha said. He reminds you that real control does not lie in your smooth shifting or the way you weave through traffic. Real control lies in the mind, steering yourself away from anger. We should drive our lives like our cars. And we should drive our cars with control. I have heard it said the best way to test a spiritual teacher is to go on a drive with the teacher at the wheel. Then you'll see the real self come out; then you'll see either control...or a teacher you don't want.

What would Buddha do when a friend hits him up for favors?

> *Misers certainly do not go to heaven. Fools don't like being generous. But the wise, rejoicing in giving, finds joy in the higher worlds.*

Dhammapada 270

Oh yes, make no mistake, Buddha does believe in heavens and hells. It's just that you simply live another lifetime there and then move on. Still, I imagine time passes slowly in hell. It is nice to think we might avoid that by doing something in this world. One thing to do is be generous.

We are fools to dislike generosity because only fools see the act of giving as separate from the rest of their lives. Sometimes the rewards of giving are distant in time (we don't get thanks or attention or a reciprocal present). Sometimes the rewards are distant in emotion (we give coldly but dutifully). But always the reward is there, because nothing is separate.

We might also remember that a gift is never deserved; if it were deserved it would be a payment. Do we wish to pay our family and friends? Of course not—so just give happily, and be happy when you too receive a gift you do not deserve.

What would Buddha do when criticized?

> *Look upon one who tells you your faults as giving you*
> *a hidden treasure, as a wise person who shows you*
> *the dangers of life. Follow that person: if you do, you*
> *will see good and not evil.*

Dhammapada 76

Buddha knows who we should be hanging with: not sycophants, some-times not even those who love us and let us slide. A real critic is a bless-ing. A person like that shows us how we really are. This is a rare oppor-tunity and we shouldn't miss out. Right.

The trick is to be open. There's nothing like criticism to bring out the monkey mind of the defensive self. The monkey mind will chatter back in the nastiest way. And you should see the things it throws. Buddha challenges us not to be this way. Are you ready for critique? How about this: Why are you reading this book when you could be donating blood?

What would Buddha do when bored?

> *If you find one thing boring,*
> *you'll find everything boring.*
>
> ### Dogen, "Guidelines for Studying the Way"

Boredom lies in our character, not in the world. "If you're bored," I've heard it said, "you're boring." Think about this.

When you're bored, you tend to bore others. Conversely, when you're bored, it is because you are boring: you are the one who engages in the act of boring. It's not the world that is boring you, it is you who are boring the world. This is Buddha's meaning.

So, when you are boring, stop doing it. Look inside and ask yourself, "Why am I draining the life from this moment?" Answering this question restores you and the world to life. Boredom becomes impossible.

What would Buddha do when fearing personal failure?

> *Am I strong enough to save the world?... Remembering all he had heard, he thought again and resolved, "I will teach the truth for the sake of saving the world."*

> **Buddhacharita 15.81-82**

It is hard to think of Buddha as having doubts, especially after his awakening, but Buddha was just a person and all persons, even enlightened ones, have doubts. He thought about the enormity of his goal—saving the world and all living things!—and asked himself, "Do I really have the strength to accomplish this?" He found the answer was yes, and he followed his duty. (Interestingly, the Sanskrit word for "duty," *dharma*, also means "teaching" and "truth.")

When we face the greatest challenges, even when we know we are right—*especially* when we know we are right—we may feel acutely conscious of the greatness of our aspiration and the smallness of our ability. Like Buddha, we must draw on everything we know, find our resolution and, like him, throw ourselves into our dharma.

Our dharma may not compare to Buddha's in scale, but it remains our duty, and if we let it teach us it will become our truth.

Toward a
New Me

So you've made it through the first section of the book. Good for you! Less critique now. Instead, this section focuses on dealing with problems that often bring out our worst, rather than our best. Here we move away from our faults and toward our potential. We herald the birth of the New Me.

Well, it's not so grand as all that, but if we can react to problems with a good heart and a good mind, we really do become better people. Buddha reminds us that we, like everything else, are not truly enduring. The person you were as a kid, even the person you were last year, is not the same person you are now. You've changed, and you're still changing. When you act mindfully and with compassion, you become something greater than you were. For that moment, you become Buddha.

Of course we slip back, but if we continually try to act as Buddhas, we continually are being reborn as Buddhas. I bow to our great effort.

What would Buddha do about changing other people?

> *Do not examine the limitations of others. Examine how you can change your own.*
>
> **Dakini Teachings 1**

So brief and so powerful, this is a lightning strike of wisdom. It sure lights me up, anyway. We never get anywhere dwelling on changing others, yet we indulge in it all the time. It's our excuse for not changing ourselves. This is why the most annoying limitations of other people just happen to be exactly the ones we have too.

When I teach college classes, I must examine the limitations of my students. In doing so, I try to teach them to do this themselves. If I fail them (sometimes literally), I have failed myself. Looking briefly at their limitations, I see deeply into my own. Even when we must attend to others' limitations, we learn most when we turn the examination to ours. Changing ourselves is not only the best way to help ourselves, it is the best way to help others.

What would Buddha do to hold his tongue?

Surely a person is born with an axe in her mouth, and she cuts herself with it when she speaks foolish words.

Sutta Nipata 657

We've all heard the expression "she has a sharp tongue" or the comment that something "cuts both ways." Have you ever put these two together in your mind? That is what Buddha does with this striking metaphor. He calls our tongue a sharp weapon that cuts both ways: it cuts the speaker along with the wielder.

When we consider that we injure ourselves by speaking foolish or hurtful words, we should summon the wisdom to keep our mouths shut. Buddha deeply realized the unity of self and other; this is why he never spoke ill of anyone, even people who slandered him. He also realized the emptiness of idle talk when real work needs to be done (by the way, this is *always*). He had gone beyond the temptation of speaking foolish words. He knew that doing so injures everyone by leading to anger and wasting time. We may not always be in touch with our Buddha Nature, but we can always feel that axe in our mouths. Remembering that, we can sometimes remain silent.

What would Buddha do about the distractions of modern life?

> Tiantong said, "If you haven't understood, you get involved in everything around you."
>
> Master Yunmen countered, "If you have understood, you get involved in everything around you!"

Record of Yunmen, Pilgrimage Record 284

We all get distracted by little things. We feel we should be pursuing this or that Big Plan, yet we get swept away in the current of events. (Perhaps this sweeping is why we *call* them "current" events.) As the adage goes: "Life is what happens to you while you're making other plans."

In this dialogue, two Zen masters explore this question of distraction. Tiantong expresses what I've just written, this sense we have that distraction is a problem. Yunmen of course knows this is true. But rather than simply agreeing with that important but obvious truth, he counters with something deeper. He says if you have truly understood reality, you *still* get involved in all the distractions of life because they are truly what life is. Life is lived in the present moment, with all its richness, its blooming, buzzing confusion. If we aren't involved in the distractions, we aren't involved at all.

By the way, this doesn't mean you have to drop the Big Plan. Just remember the Big Plan is made up of little experiences.

What would Buddha do to avoid burnout?

*Moderate effort over a long time is important, no matter
what you are trying to do. One brings failure on oneself
by working extremely hard at the beginning, attempting
to do too much, and then giving it all up after a short
time.*

The Dalai Lama

Life is long when we have a difficult task to do. We'd love to just leap
into it and accomplish the whole thing in one inspired flash. This is not
the way of the world. Instead, we must marshal our strength for the long
haul, whether the task is spiritual or political.

The Dalai Lama has earned the right to say these words. Look at
his unending efforts to save the Tibetan people and their culture from
the Chinese occupation of their homeland. If we value our causes we owe
it to them not to fail, since our own failure breeds failure in those who
follow us. If we cannot carry the torch to the goal, it is so much better to
pass the torch than to have it flare up and then flame out in our hands.

What would Buddha do about closed-minded people?

People with small minds want a small Law because they can't believe they could become Buddha.

Lotus Sutra 2

Where does intolerance begin? It starts with the pettiness that forces people to believe others are just as petty. Small-minded people feel they need strict laws to keep the peace and detailed codes of conduct because they can't be trusted to be good. They demean themselves and so demean others.

Buddha saw things differently. He had an open mind about people. He taught us to believe the best of ourselves and embrace a wider truth because we have the potential to become Buddha. Buddha saw our potential, our awakened nature. Because of this, he taught a "large Law," one of acceptance and trust. Where does acceptance begin? We need to think like Buddha, to open our own minds and begin to promote good in others. As we trust our own good nature, we will trust others.

What would Buddha do when ganged up on?

Some would take sticks or tiles and stones and hit him. But running away he would still call out, "I will never condemn you, for you are all certain to become Buddhas!"

Lotus Sutra 20

Here Buddha describes a bodhisattva named "Never Condemning," who faced the most brutal treatment without ever losing his perspective. Though people beat him, he kept crying out their future: they would become Buddhas.

How did Never Condemning keep his head? He never lost sight of the big picture—that all beings are Buddha and some day will act that way. With his remarkable courage and confidence, he finally got through to his attackers and they listened to his teaching.

Those of us lucky enough not to face beatings still sometimes lose our perspective. We need to emulate this wise one and keep in mind that we too shall overcome, someday. With that perspective and enough patience, we can stay positive no matter what befalls us.

What would Buddha do if he could afford to give only a little?

> *If a confused and distracted person took even a single flower and offered it to a Buddha image, he would come to see countless Buddhas.*

Lotus Sutra 2

Offering something to a Buddha image is sacred, but what matters is the intention rather than the size of the offering. When you give what you have, the gift is good, no matter how humble. Jesus said the pennies of the poor widow were a greater offering than the riches of the wealthy. Buddha is saying the same thing here.

As with sacred gifts, so with secular ones. No matter how little we have to offer, when we can give, we should give. Travelling through Asia, I saw the humblest offerings at shrines and myself received small tokens from the poor. Giving a flower, receiving a flower, this is the greatest delight. When this happens, giver and receiver both see Buddhas all around.

What would Buddha do about getting angry at fools?

> *Some people are like big children, harming others*
> *without even seeing it. Staying angry with these fools*
> *is like being mad at fire because it burns.*

> **Bodhicharyavatara 6.39**

Not everyone grows up, no matter how old they get. Some people just go around wrecking things, sometimes for the spite of it. Other times they simply don't understand they've done any harm. Of course we get upset with them, and perhaps an immediate word or shout helps (it helps us, anyway). These people are like kids or pets; it is their nature to cause trouble.

Buddha's wisdom here is to separate your swift censure from your lasting anger. When disciplining a young child, you need to do it as soon as possible. With a pet it must be right away. After a few hours it's all forgotten by them, and it ought to be forgotten by you, too. Should you hit a child in anger? Of course not; but hitting a child in delayed justice is even worse.

What would Buddha do to be on time?

You may think time is passing you by and not realize time never even gets here.... People only notice time going by and don't deeply see that the reality of time lives in every moment.

Dogen, "Being-time," Shobogenzo

Zen Master Dogen, in his unique language, tries to awaken us to this very moment. What is time? Or perhaps—when is time? Time is now; now is both what and when. In this sense we are always on time. Where else would we be? Be in this moment. Start now.

Being in this moment benefits us and the world. We feel time is passing us by too fast when we're not in the flow of time. This is when we run late. Don't wait for the moment to get here; it doesn't arrive. Instead, realize your presence in this moment, for the time-being. When you remove your separation from time, you'll be on time more often.

What would Buddha do when making a salad?

> Picking up a green leaf, turn it into Buddha's body; taking Buddha's body, turn it into a green leaf. This is the wondrous process of saving all living things.

> **Dogen, "Instructions for the Cook," Shobogenzo**

Although we like to say simple pleasures are the best and claim we love people who are the salt of the earth, most of us do not act this way. We might think all things are part of a blessed creation, but we don't treat them as such. Buddha's teaching asks us to practice what we preach.

If Buddha can be found in a simple leaf, well, Buddha must be everywhere. Buddhist scriptures tell us over and over that all things are Buddha's body. The trick is seeing them that way. Dogen emphasizes that this is practice and awakening at once: when we treat the leaf as Buddha we won't need to give special care to Buddha's body since we already lavish that care on the whole world. Acting this way is acting as Buddha; acting as Buddha we are Buddhas. Being Buddhas we save all living things. It starts with the leaf.

What would Buddha do if he feels sleepy while reading this book?

Just be normal, without trying to act any special way. Move your bowels, piss, put on your clothes, eat your food, and lie down when you're tired.

Record of Linji 13

When we're trying to be spiritual, we tend to neglect the body, even deny it. Buddha does not recommend this; we are not to follow a path of renunciation. In fact, as Buddhism has developed, the teaching has more and more embraced the body as the carrier of Buddha, as Buddha itself.

Zen Master Linji insists that we just be who we are. There is no need to pretend you are not full of shit, both mental and physical. Simply act in accordance with the dictates of your body. Don't try to fool anyone into thinking your body is pure or that you can function without it. Your body has great wisdom in it; treat it right and don't be embarrassed by it.

What would Buddha do when waiting in the snow for a taxi?

> A monk asked, "What does it mean to go where there's no cold and no heat?"
>
> Tung-shan said, "In the cold, cold freezes you; in the heat, heat burns you up."

Blue Cliff Record 43

This exchange forms the culmination of a famous koan, a Zen story designed to awaken the student to reality. Not having solved the koan myself, I cannot solve it for you, but I can tell you about the Buddhist truth it expresses.

Zen teacher Tung-shan is telling the monk to break down the gap between self and physical feelings. When simple feeling fills the experience, the self drops away. In this moment physical discomfort drops away along with the self. The cold freezes you to death. The heat burns you to death. The death frees you from yourself. This Zen teaching goes back to Buddha's fundamental awakening from the dream of the self.

Next time you're suffering from heat or cold or wind or headache, whatever the feeling, just feel it without evaluation. Relax. Let it kill you. Even a beginner can make this work.

What would Buddha do to discipline an employee?

> *The right time to show your good character is when you are pestered by somebody weaker than you.*

> *Jatakamala 33.13*

When someone stronger harms you, there is no great virtue in stopping yourself from lashing back. You know that doing so would be stupid. When someone of equal strength hurts you and you don't react, you are beginning to show wisdom and intelligence. But refraining from acting against someone weaker, who can do little damage to you, is a true test of character.

When with impunity you can punish someone who deserves it, you are faced with a powerful question. Do you act with justice or mercy? You can be the instrument of pain or love. Buddha tells us to choose love. Why? Not just to be nice, but because retribution furthers pain in the world, whereas mercy stops pain and furthers compassion. Rather than being a pawn of anger and generating new waves of hostility, you can create waves of compassion in their place. You will do yourself good and maybe change the person who has harmed you. This is *real* corporate culture.

What would Buddha do if he feels that life is passing him by?

Attention is living; inattention is dying. The attentive never stop; the inattentive are dead already.

Dhammapada 21

We frequently hear it said that staying involved in life keeps you young. In these pithy words, Buddha explains why.

Attention, mindfulness, vigilance keeps us involved in the current of life and in the very moment we are experiencing now. Without that attention, we immediately die to the moment and slowly die to all other things. When we are inattentive we miss out on life itself: not just the lives around us, but our own as well.

At the highest level, when we attend entirely to life, there is no longer any room even for the illusion of our selves. Living with this attention, there truly is no dying, since the self is simply seen through. I'm not sure I'll ever get to this level, but the effort itself brings me to life.

Pure Love

"Oh, 'tis love, 'tis love, that makes the world go round!" said the Duchess in *Alice in Wonderland*, paraphrasing a line from Dante's *Divine Comedy*. So long as we have ears to hear and eyes to see, so long will love lead the rhythm of the world. And what lover has not felt the earth move and seen the stars dance in shared joy?

But love—whether kept or lost, whether found in the contraction of two souls into one or the expansion of one into the whole cosmos—really is a comedy. We try to love, but we so often fail. We fail in the finding. We fail in the keeping. We fail in the understanding, the sharing, the losing. We fail again and again and yet we smile and come back to try again. This is the very stuff of comedy: so human, so endearing, so beautiful.

Many people misunderstand Buddha's words on love. Buddha never forbade us love, he only reminded us that love leads to attachment and attachment leads to suffering. The life of a recluse is not for the many. As for us, even for the most deluded, life with love beats life with lack. In reading this section, I hope you can find questions and answers that help you to love and even to enjoy the process of learning to love.

What would Buddha do when a loved one moves away?

As shooting stars, a blindness, as a lamp,
A magic trick, as dewdrops, or a bubble,
As a dream, a lightning flash, or cloud,
So should we view all that is conditioned.

Diamond Sutra 32

Here Buddha speaks of the fleeting nature of all things that are conditioned, built up of many parts. Our loves, our lives, even our selves are this way. When our revels are ended, what is left? Only this awareness that they were all as a dream and have melted into air.

We like to see shooting stars and magic tricks, but we must enjoy them while they are happening. After all, isn't its brevity what makes a shooting star so special? We don't expect it to endure and we shouldn't expect the pleasure of company to endure. When we're missing people, we're missing the moments we shared together, moments which by their very nature must pass away. Only the passing of the old moments allows new moments to occur. We need to return to the present to experience them. Buddha did this and thus fully lived his life. Time for us to do the same.

What would Buddha do when a loved one dies?

Not through weeping and grief do we obtain peace of mind. We increase misery; we harm our bodies. We become thin and pale, destroying ourselves by our own power.

Sutta Nipata 584

There are times when we must weep if we are to remain human, when our feelings demand expression, whether that expression brings embarrassment or tears to those who watch. Buddha knew this; this is not what he counsels against here. When a life ends we do need to mourn. But once we have faced and expressed our grief, we have to let it go.

This is the rub, because we hold on to grief. We hold on to it as we held on to the one whose loss prompts the grief. This holding drains us and prevents our directing that energy toward someone new. We remain attached to those we love. The Japanese poet Issa wrote this haiku on the death of his daughter: "This dewdrop world, / it *is* a dewdrop world; / and yet, and yet…"

How he longs for permanence! But he won't find any; nor will we. Yet if his tears will not bring back his child, maybe his verse will return him and us to an awareness of how things really are. His grief, even this will pass away.

What would Buddha do to be a good husband or boyfriend?

In five ways should a husband minister to his wife: by respecting her, by being kind to her, by being faithful to her, by giving her authority, by adorning her.

Digha Nikaya 31

Before expanding on Buddha's advice, I must first admit how abjectly he himself failed to follow it. He abandoned his own wife and infant son to follow the path of renunciation. What are we to make of that? Surely he caused them great suffering. Yet he had been pressured into marrying against his will, and the tradition tells us he did come back to convert them to Buddhism and guide them to awakening. It is so hard to judge the choices of any young person; we should be cautious in judging Buddha.

Buddha's advice remains strikingly contemporary today, after 2500 years. Look at what these five ways of caring for one's wife center on: giving attention to her as a person both lovable and competent. To one's wife one gives love and fidelity, but also authority. Such advice, shocking in ancient times, is now simply mandatory, and it comes in stark contrast to the words of the New Testament. Both religions promote love, but here there is no hint of hierarchy, and the focus falls on the husband's emotional vows to his wife.

What would Buddha do to be a good wife or girlfriend?

> *In five ways should a wife, ministered to by her husband...love him: by performing her duties well, by giving hospitality to their relatives, by being faithful to him, by supervising their money, and by skillfully doing all her work.*

Digha Nikaya 31

Here is the second half of Buddha's advice for the marriage pair. What strikes us here? The remarkable focus on the wife's duties as worldly partner. How is the wife to love her husband? By taking charge of many of the couple's responsibilities.

The wife's duties move her powerfully out into the world, not merely in relationships, but in various kinds of work. Specifically Buddha mentions her being in charge of the money. The picture here focuses on competence and command. In contrast to the husband's emotional duties, Buddha emphasizes the wife's organizational duties.

Notice that only one requirement is made of both husband and wife: they must each be faithful. Only in that integrity and commitment can a lasting relationship blossom.

What would Buddha do about parents who don't understand?

All parents naturally love the words of their beloved children, but they don't change their minds.

Jataka 544

It is difficult to change anyone's mind about anything. How much more so a parent. After all, when a child is old enough to intelligently disagree with a parent, the parent is even older. Your parents remember you when you were a know-nothing little imp. In fact they remember the world before you were even born, and it seemed to get along just fine without your wisdom, thank you very much.

Your parents love you, and you have no doubt taught them many things, but to change their minds about something important is one of the most difficult things in the world. In this situation it is good to remember two things. First, just as your life is your own to live, their lives are their own. Perhaps you can let them keep their own minds. Second, as Buddha hints, they naturally love you and want you to be happy. If you really need to change their minds, don't do it through words—do it by showing them how happy your way of thinking makes you over time.

What would Buddha do to care for aging parents?

> *Once I was supported by them; now I will be their support. I will perform the duties they performed and maintain the family and its traditions. I will preserve my inheritance and make myself worthy of my heritage.*

> **Digha Nikaya 31**

"Once I was supported by them; now I will be their support." Such a beautiful line and sentiment, but so hard to manage today. Buddha's meaning is unmistakable: a child's duty to her parents never dies. As older people continue to live longer, we face this duty earlier and carry it longer than ever before. When Buddha lived, parents died only a few years after retirement. Now they may live decades—and we hope they do. But few countries are well-prepared to respond to this, and few businesses have provided enough for it. So the burden remains with the family. If the parents cannot support themselves, the children must take over.

Look again at Buddha's words; he does not stop with maintaining one's parents. The child's duties extend to maintaining the very idea of the family itself. In these days of debate over "family values," Buddha does not give us specifics; he gives us principles. Our duties lie in maintaining traditions and making ourselves worthy of them. The deepest way to honor our parents is to carry their heritage into the future.

What would Buddha do in a family crisis?

The family stands together like a forest,
While storms blow down the tree that stands alone.

Jataka 74

Buddha reminds us we're not so different from other living things, even trees. He uses the metaphor of trees—natural, rooted and deeply powerful.

Like a group of trees that, standing together, support each other against any wind, so should every family stand in the face of any storm that threatens them. A single person is like a lonely tree; he faces the wind alone and can be broken. But a family that supports each other is much stronger than each member alone. Trees in a forest extend their limbs toward each other; this is how they hold one another up in a storm. This is not so different from families, is it? Don't we also extend our arms toward each other, and hold each other up in a crisis?

Standing together can be difficult in such times. Your roots can get crowded, your sun can get blocked. This can be frustrating, even painful. But if you support your family, they will support you, and the strength you have together is the greatest on this earth.

What would Buddha do if his child misbehaves?

Misbehaving children irritate you no end. But you tolerate your own child's bad behavior because she's "yours."

Bankei, The Hoshinji Sermons

Why do we let our own children get away with so much obnoxious behavior? Because, as Bankei hints, we think of them as extensions of ourselves. We don't want to make them feel bad. That's the good side of our indulgence. We also don't want them to have limits. That's the bad side, because limits are unavoidable and we need to live by them. A parent who fails to teach limits to a child creates a most unhappy environment around the child and eventually creates a most unhappy child. We must learn to say, "No."

Buddha does not want us to crush our kids' spirits. Rather, he cautions us to foster their awareness that happiness and satisfaction come from inside, not outside. Too many of us act as if children cannot comprehend this. Naturally children have a hard time accepting it, so just as naturally we had better expose them to the idea as early as possible. Not letting children run your life is an aspect of this. Not trying to create happiness through indulgence is another. Showing children that their parents live by this principle may be the most important aspect of all.

What would Buddha do when family comes to visit?

Treating family as well as you can when they come to visit is good and fortunate because it leads to good here and in the next world.

**Mangalasutra Atuva,
Saddharmaratnavaliya**

We all know how difficult family can be, especially around the holidays when everyone is together for an eternity. When relatives descend like locusts, Buddha does not demand we be perfect hosts. What he tells us is twofold. First, treat your family as well as you can. This is obvious and we should give no less. Second, your efforts will be rewarded, not only in the blessings of a happier family but in a future you can't even imagine.

This is a lovely thought. Even if, like me, you doubt a personal afterlife, you can see Buddha's point. Your family carries on after you. They create the next world. Be good to them and that world will be a better place, no matter what world it is. In this way the good we do at home spreads down through the generations.

What would Buddha do when people compete for his attention?

> *"If a couple has seven children and one gets sick, though they love each child the same, the parents think most about the sick child." Just like parents who think most about the sick child, Buddha thinks most about an evil man.*

> **Nichiren, "Winter Always Turns to Spring"**

Buddha loves all people, but he wouldn't spend an equal amount of time with each. He naturally spent his time with the sick, not the healthy. Jesus described his own ministry similarly. This may not seem fair, but it expresses love. Nichiren compares Buddha to loving parents. They are like doctors, but even more involved and supportive when a child needs attention. This is not favoritism, simply good parenting.

When parents give extra time to one child, they cannot give it to others. This situation can grow difficult. When one child is seriously ill, the need for attention may last years. In a crisis, not only children need special consideration. Sometimes even friends vie for attention you can't give to each one. What can you do? The answer lies in love. When each child or friend knows you love them, they can wait for their share of attention. This doesn't mean they will like the wait—it means they can handle it.

What would Buddha do to strengthen a friendship?

> *A friend in need walks seven steps to help us.*
> *A real comrade walks twelve to give us aid.*
> *A person walking weeks with us is kin;*
> *Walking longer they become ourself.*

Jataka 83

Perhaps the question could be changed to "What *wouldn't* Buddha do to strengthen a friendship?" since he would do so much. Walking with our friends when they need us, we grow closer. Buddha tells us when friends need something, we should give it, not just to gratify them, but to make a connection to something deeper in both them and ourselves.

Buddha emphasizes how that connection between friends should be fostered since it reveals what we really are. After all, what is a friend but a person in whom we see the underlying unity of all living things? We love our friends because we understand them, we share with them, we feel connected to them. Aiding friendship leads to comradeship, which then leads to kinship, which eventually reveals that the separate selves of friends and us are not really separate at all. Walking together, being there for each other, we realize we cannot be ourselves apart from them.

What would Buddha do if a friend is abusing drugs?

> *When someone goes wrong, it is right for his real friends to move him, even by force, to do the right thing.*

> **Jatakamala 20.23**

Our modern world puts us under great pressure. It also offers many good means for escaping that pressure. Weekends, good films, parks, healthy food, time with family—all these relax us, allowing us to face again the pressure of responsibilities. The world also provides addictive and dangerous means for escaping pressure: legal and illegal drugs, violent or abusive behavior, depression—the list goes on. We have all seen friends go down these roads. Have we been friends to them in their need?

Buddha never heard the term "intervention," but that is exactly what he demands with these words. Even if it sometimes takes force, we should try to help our friends when their strength to help themselves is exhausted. This may be the hardest task in the world (other than helping ourselves). It is usually the least-rewarded as well. It is also deeply holy.

What would Buddha do to understand his relationship with his fellow creatures?

Of all living creatures, not a single one has not been your father or mother. So as a way of repaying the kindness of those creatures, set out to work for their welfare.

Dakini Teachings 1

This world is very old, older than we can conceive. Buddhism teaches that in the count of years and through the process of reincarnation, every living person and animal has been your mother or father at least once. The love they showed you in those lifetimes still needs to be repaid. You must honor and love them by working to help them.

This teaching lies at the very origin of Tibetan Buddhism, coming from the mouth of the great bodhisattva, Padmasambhava. He does not expect us to save the souls of all living things, but simply to work "for their welfare." In his great compassion, he advocates doing whatever is needed for the well-being of the biosphere. Even if we do not believe in reincarnation, this practice may let us return the love of every living person and animal by being each one's parent. In the meantime, what a lovely way to awaken our love for our fellow creatures.

What would Buddha do to help others?

He gives rise to this pure thought: "I will never abandon any living thing. I will love all living things as one. I will lead all living things to nirvana!"

18,000 Verse Perfection of Wisdom Sutra 11

Time after time, incarnation after incarnation, Buddha gives everything, even his life, to help others. But if we are not Buddhas what can we do? Buddha calls us to be bodhisattvas, compassionate beings who stay here in this broken world to help all living things. The words above describe the ideal to which we should aspire.

Such is the total commitment of the bodhisattva, who devotes his or her life and future to saving all living things. Yes, that sounds awfully holy, but millions of Buddhists all over the world repeat this vow: "Living things are numberless; I vow to save them all." Start with yourself and great compassion may take hold of you, too.

Lust
for Life

Ah, here's the juice! To grab and hold and "tear our pleasures with rough strife, through the iron gates of life." Here's where we feast and drink, where we clasp and melt and disappear into our joys. All this sounds so good, so deliriously good, but in our delirium we also cause pain. Why is this?

More strongly than with any other teaching, Buddha warned us against this delirium, for the madness of love so easily slips into the insanity of lust. Not merely the lust of sex, but the lust of all the appetites inevitably brings us pain. At first flush we don't know when the pain will come, but it will. Sometimes at once, as with food; sometimes when we slink away, as from a tryst; sometimes when our whole lives slink away from us, as with drugs.

So we ask, how can we enjoy this physical world, and our physical selves in it, without causing our own ruin. Does this sound melodramatic? It might, but in fact this is a battle we fight every day. Our desires are infinite, unquenchable, impossible, and our lives can never be. Buddha can help us resolve this conflict. His words in this section lead us toward the very heart of his teaching, the wisdom that transcends desire.

What would Buddha do about lust?

An older man brings home a girl with breasts like fruit.
He can't sleep for jealousy. This leads to his downfall.

Sutta Nipata 110

We've all seen this couple. Older men with younger women. What do these couples have in common? Being in the thrall of pleasures. The specifics of pleasure don't matter to Buddha. What matters is the misery we feel when we pine for pleasure, when we lose pleasure or miss it, even when—like the man here—we have pleasure but suffer as we struggle to keep it.

Who does not live like this? I'm typing these words on a new computer. I paid a lot of money for this computer. I'm careful with it. I paid a full day's wages just for the insurance on it, a vain attempt to ward off its eventual demise. I actually caught myself wondering if I should use it today, since I didn't want to harm it by taking it outside. It's a laptop, for goodness' sake! Am I not like the man who worries all night about how to keep that girl to himself? Is that how he imagined his nights with her? (What does she talk about with him?) Yes, my lust for this computer might lead to failure. After all, computer lust and sexual lust are not that different. Look at the language: full of hard drives, and RAM, and numbers of strokes, and having the biggest whatever-it-is (and being seen with it). Buddha would tell us to live with what we have and accept both its coming and its going.

What would Buddha do about adultery?

> *Whatever fame and reputation he had before, of course vanishes…. In the grip of his fantasies, he broods like a fool. Hearing the outrage of others, he gets depressed. Urged on by others, he then becomes his own worst enemy. This indeed is his great affair. He falls into his own lies.*

> **Sutta Nipata 817-819**

Of course reading this one cannot help but think of the pitiful escapades of American presidents and other politicos. This is a common pattern of the sexually driven, but it seems a special predilection of those, like politicians, desperate for public accolades and private attentions.

We might ask ourselves what President Clinton's legacy and reputation might have been without his juvenile and crippling sexual scandals. But perhaps more important, we must try to learn from his behavior. Are we not all, like him, deeply conflicted about sex: liberated yet prudish; voyeuristic yet private; publicly awash in sex, yet privately often narrow or compulsive. Do we wish to gain and lose our leaders (and ourselves) on this level? And what about friends? Buddha wouldn't condone adultery, but neither would he abandon the adulterer.

What would Buddha do about getting drunk?

There are six results of drinking: decreasing wealth, increasing quarrels, danger of disease, gaining an evil reputation, indecent exposure, and ruining intelligence.

Digha Nikaya 31

Buddha never tired of reminding us that every action produces consequences. Drinking may give pleasure in the moment, but getting drunk often enough leads to these six unfortunate outcomes.

Does this mean Buddha rejected all drinking? Only in his rules for monks and nuns. For the great majority of us, the precept to follow is closer to "Do not abuse intoxicants."

But what is abuse? That we have to decide for ourselves. Now that we know red wine helps our hearts, a glass of syrah (or zinfandel, or cabernet, the list is long and enticing) doesn't seem like abuse, it may even be "medicinal." Each person must ask the question, "What does this wine do to my mindfulness? Can I drink this glass and stay aware, stay awakened?" When the answer is no, we must stop. Not abusing drink and drugs is a precept for everyone.

What would Buddha do about that coffee habit?

> *Our country is full of sickly-looking, skinny people, just because we don't drink tea. Whenever people feel weak, they should drink tea.*
>
> **Kissa Yojoki**

Sorry to break it to all you java-junkies, but coffee addiction, like any other addiction, is not something Buddha would endorse. Yes, it gets you going; and, yes, it may be a morning ritual, but you can't get going without it, and that particular ritual does not count as a meditation, even if it takes half an hour and you do it every day and feel it is an obligation.

The Buddhist quote above suggests you drink tea, especially green tea, instead of coffee. Tea is, after all, by far the most popular beverage in the world, other than water, and it's healthy. But even tea can become an addiction. When we have to have something, the truth is that thing *has us*. Ask yourself who is master, you or those things you "need." If it's not you, something is wrong.

What would Buddha do about material possessions?

See them floundering after their cherished possessions,
like fish flopping in a river starved of water.

Sutta Nipata 777

Buddha compares us to these tragic fish, gasping in the brutal air, frantically looking for heaven-knows-what. Are we searching for deeper water? Are we struggling to snatch the last shred of food? Most pitiful of all, are we aggressively defending some useless possession in the very face of death?

We are some spectacle, I no less than the rest of us! I've told you about my computer—wait until you hear about my house and car. Meanwhile I age, I slowly die, but I continue to vainly thrash around. We have got to remember, the real possession is life itself, and even that is only on loan. Buddha doesn't say we cannot enjoy the beautiful things we are lucky enough to have. He does say we should not let them distract us from our real job: awakening to our life and death.

What would Buddha do about "The American Dream"?

> *Since this world passes away, with everyone fooling everyone—it is unwise to think of anything as yours in the midst of this intermingling, this dream.*
>
> ***Buddhacharita 6.48***

What makes something ours? Money? But what makes money ours? I can understand owning something as simple as food. But who owns it once I've eaten it? And let's not even talk about owning property. How can a person, who lasts 80 years, own a piece of the earth, which endures for millions of millennia?

I just don't understand property, though I have to admit that once something feels like it's mine I really want to keep it. But everything I own will pass away, or I will pass away first and the thing will be someone else's. In this time of confusion (beautiful word: all things fused together), in this dream where nothing lasts, we should think of things as confused. Even our very bodies are confused; our minds, too (especially our minds). Don't cling to the stuff of dreams; let it flow.

What would Buddha do if his credit cards are maxed out?

Once they've gained all the lands on one side of the sea, kings want to conquer the other side. As rivers never fill the ocean, pleasures never satisfy people.

Buddhacharita 11.12

After conquering all the known world, Alexander the Great lamented there were no more lands to conquer. Yet he did not even live to govern the lands he already had. This is crazy, but we are all like this Greek conqueror. We never feel satisfied. Ambitious people can't enjoy what they have, driven by their need to attain more. Lazy people like what they've got, but they sure would like more, in case the things they have run out.

Buddhism teaches we will never be satisfied until we stop thinking like this. We must break the delusion that our separate selves can be happy apart from the infinite world that surrounds us. It is like thinking we are the ocean, drinking the rivers of the world but never being full. Only when we realize we are the whole biosphere will we be happy. We are the thirsty ocean; we are the sweet rivers too.

What would Buddha do to gain health, beauty, happiness, status, heaven?

> *It's not right for the good person who desires happiness to pray for it.... Instead, the good person who desires happiness should walk the path of practice leading to happiness.*

Anguttara Nikaya 5.43

Buddha repeats these words for health, beauty, status, and the attainment of heaven. We don't get these things through prayer, or at least we shouldn't try to get them that way. Of course there is something in us that wants these things now, wants them the easy way. Buddha probably did believe prayer works, but that does not mean the result is always satisfactory.

This is one of the great psychological insights of Buddha. What we gain without effort does not satisfy like what comes through the sweat of our brow or the work of self-transformation. No berries taste as sweet as those we pick. No insight changes us as deeply as what we discover ourselves. Prayer might help, but walking the endless path of practice is the only way to a deep reward. Sometimes just the path is reward enough.

What would Buddha do when deciding where to go for dinner?

Whether the food is peasant or gourmet,
Long-prepared or merely made in haste,
Served on silver or on wooden tray,
Love makes the meal to everybody's taste.

Jatakas 346

Perhaps this is not a big question for many of you. Maybe food is not an important part of your life. Ah, but let me remind you that of all pleasures, food is most central, most necessary, most accessible and reliable. Further, being most frequent it gives us the greatest opportunity for spiritual practice. Rejoice in your food and follow Buddha's advice on how to enjoy it!

Here Buddha gives us a fundamental recipe for culinary and other pleasures: enjoy them with others in an atmosphere of love. Love reminds all present that true pleasure is shared pleasure. Then, even though the occasion may seem lacking, the experience can be as rich as we have power to experience. For me, the simplest food often proves the most sublime, so long as I share it with my wife.

What would Buddha do to allow himself sexual pleasure?

When one chants "Namu-myoho-renge-kyo," then, even during love-making, the passions are awakening and the sufferings of life and death are nirvana.

Nichiren, "Passions are Awakening"

This is—if you will forgive me—hardcore Mahayana teaching. Nichiren deeply believes that since we are already Buddha, and since nirvana is present right here in this world, even our passions express the pure nature of reality. This means if we hold our Buddha nature firmly in mind, even our most passionate actions will remain awakened. Nichiren did this by repeating his famous mantra, but there are many other ways.

I personally find this teaching joyful, affirmative, and a great relief! I am simply not at the stage where I can give up my passions. I think most of you are with me on this one. But I do want to free myself from attachment and delusion. Thankfully, Buddha meets us halfway. We love making love (or eating barbecue potato chips, or whatever); that's okay. Just try to preserve your Buddha nature while you enjoy these passions. Think of others, recite a mantra, radiate loving-kindness, remember your breathing. Buddha gives us many ways to do this; we can also make up our own. As we work to become Buddha, this is plenty hard spiritual practice.

What would Buddha do when he can't resist having dessert?

Enjoying the senses, she stays clean of them. She picks the lotus without getting wet. She has reached the root and capers free of senses even while indulging them.

Saraha, Dohakosha 64

We all indulge ourselves sometimes. Buddha understands. When we fulfill desires we have to try to remain undefiled by them. We have to use the power of desire itself to move us toward awakening. How? By staying mindful of their power over us and our actions as we consummate them. Don't possess another; mutually please each other. Don't wolf the chocolate; think of the labor that brought it to you. When we really experience our desires and fulfillments, we realize oneness with the Buddha way.

What would Buddha do about prostitution?

Sometimes he becomes a prostitute, one who lures those people prone to lust, leading them on with desire, but then leading them forward onto Buddha's path.

Vimalakirti Sutra 7

Buddha never condemns prostitution any more than other jobs that lead to suffering. I'm sure he would condemn working at a fast-food joint that causes destruction to the rainforest. The harm caused by the job is what matters; for Buddha, manufacturing nerve gas, though legal, is vastly worse than turning tricks, though illegal.

Buddha does not actually favor prostitution. It causes harm, deceit and disease; it ensnares the lustful while weakening the power of love. Yet in this saying the bodhisattva becomes a prostitute to help others. It *is* possible to fight lust with lust. This tells us the path to wisdom can lead through pleasure. Selling one's body is not like selling a weapon. It may be risky and tainted, but if a bodhisattva can do it, it is not forbidden.

Doing the
Right Thing

What is morality? What does it mean to do the right thing? It seems it should be easy to know, if hard to do. But in the real world, it is often mercilessly difficult even to figure out the standards we then fail to live up to. This section of the book helps us find those standards for ourselves, drawing on those first upheld by Buddha.

Buddha often wrestled with questions of morality. His own conscience and his sincere followers demanded it. That is the path of every founder of a religion. We have many questions of right and wrong and Buddha spoke many times addressing them. Indeed, he made "right action," "right speech," and "right livelihood" the first steps on the Eightfold Noble Path. Those principles form the path for laypersons perhaps even more than for monks and nuns. The latter have elaborate codes of conduct to obey; we have only the principles and our integrity in following them. Other sections of this book have raised moral questions, but here we look directly at personal, social and global ethics. Here we ask Buddha to help us do the right thing.

What would Buddha do if a cashier gives him too much change?

When no one else is visible, it doesn't mean no one is around: I'm still there. A witness might notice me doing something wrong, but I see it much more deeply.

Jatakamala 12.15-16

There is simply no getting away with anything. Even if you do something in secrecy, someone already knows: you do. Not only do you know, you know in a powerful and insightful way. You realize the depth of your action, its motivation, severity, maybe even its repercussions.

We sometimes like to think we can get away with hidden things. On a deeper level we know this is wrong in two ways. First, because our internal witness is watching and knows all. More importantly, because deception is unworthy. We don't really want to get away with evil, even petty corruption, because we don't want anyone else to get away with it, either. This is our noble Buddha nature surfacing. Despite our usual selfish attitudes, we profoundly wish for justice and compassion.

Do you doubt our essential good nature? Then why do you think we condemn ourselves when we alone know we've done something wrong?

What would Buddha do if caught red-handed?

Though he still can act in evil ways
In his thoughts, his words, or even deeds,
He cannot conceal an evil act, and this
Shows he has attained awakened peace.

Khuddakapatha 6.11

Just as Buddha must be honest with himself, so must he not conceal his acts, whether good or bad, whether they embarrassed him or gave him pride. Buddha takes responsibility and stands up for what he does. No pretense or evasion, just the truth.

Of course Buddha is hardly going to be doing much that he'd want to conceal, but these words show how even a wise person sometimes slips. As we work to be Buddhas, let's face it, we screw up right and left. If we are clever, when we're caught we may be able to wriggle out of the external penalties. Fine, but I've found I can't elude the internal penalties. Buddha would tell us those are bad to begin with and made still worse by evading the others. This is no way to live.

What would Buddha do when he sees injustice?

> *The innocent who suffers insults, whips, and chains,*
> *whose weapon is endurance and whose army is*
> *character—that person I call holy.*

> ### Dhammapada 399

Buddha was definitely on the side of the oppressed and suffering; he had no truck with the ignorant, the greedy, and the hateful. Yet Buddha was still a man of his times. He rebelled against the religion of his day by accepting people regardless of their social station, but he did not concern himself much with politics. He was much like Jesus, who was content to give to Caesar what was Caesar's.

Buddha here admires not the revolutionary but the quiet person who stands up to injustice. In the last hundred years we have learned how to continue Buddha's rebellion in new ways. Civil Rights leader Rosa Parks sat down. The lone man in front of the tank in Tiananmen Square stood up. How are we carrying forward the social justice of Buddha?

What would Buddha do about caring for the sick?

Whoever...would tend me, should tend the sick.

Mahavagga 25.3

What a beautiful line! It calls to mind Jesus' disciples asking him when they had cared for him. Jesus replies, "Truly, I say to you, as you did it to one of the least of these my people, you did it to me" (Matthew 25:40).

What did these teachers want? Great temples? Burnt offerings? No, of course not. Sincere supplication, perhaps? Glorification of their greatness? No, not even these honors. They didn't reject them, but they didn't ask for them, either. Here is what they really ask: for us to turn our care to the world, to those who need us. There is never any shortage of need. Buddha is doing just fine—why don't we take care of someone else?

I remember a man who walked up the long stairs to my home. He was dying of AIDS and just wanted something to eat. He was Jesus. Eating with him, tending him for that time, I was a bodhisattva. If there is a judgment after this life, I hope he will be rewarded for the blessing he gave me.

What would Buddha do for the homeless?

> *He makes his body into food and drink,*
> *first relieving hunger and thirst,*
> *then teaching people the truth.*
> *Where there are those in poverty and need,*
> *he comes with unending supplies,*
> *allowing them to encourage and lead others.*

Vimalakirti Sutra 8

I find the problem of homeless people hard to face in person. I don't want to be around the abject and miserable. When near them, I wonder, should I give when I'm not sure where my gift is going?

Buddha reminds me no one learns "the truth" before eating, sleeping, and cleaning themselves up. This is simply a fact of human nature and we had better acknowledge it. As playwright Bertolt Brecht said, "First grub, then ethics." The wise and compassionate person feeds the homeless first, even lets them drink. When they are ready to turn themselves around, he encourages them, not before. So when homeless people bum a buck off you, don't be too critical. When they are ready they will lead others, not before. In the meantime, let's show some compassion.

What would Buddha do about eating meat?

> *Anger, arrogance, inflexibility, hostility,*
> *deception, envy, pride, conceit, bad company,*
> *these are impure foods, not meat.*

Sutta Nipata 245

Yes, the sutras are conflicted on this question. As with the Bible, one may find passages to support a variety of views on a single subject. Why have I chosen this one? Several powerful reasons: first, there is evidence that Buddha himself and his early disciples ate meat; that Buddhist vegetarianism only arose as a response to Hindu vegetarianism. Second, Buddhist monks eat meat to this day throughout South and Southeast Asia; even for monks the precepts allow it. Third, all Buddhists accept this text. Fourth, these words of Buddha take us to what really matters: mind.

Buddha constantly returns to mind and intention in his teaching. What matters most is what the mind takes in, feeds on, and puts back out into the world. He calls the body filthy, full of disease and dung, impossible to purify. Avoiding meat will not cleanse your body or save you from death; there is no point in attempting these things. Purity comes on another level, from a pure mind. All things must die; so long as we do not cause their deaths, we are not creating any more suffering by eating them—unless we cause that suffering in our own minds, in which case meat indeed becomes impure. Until then, like Buddha himself, we may eat.

What would Buddha do about killing?

Better conquering self than a thousand times
a thousand enemies.... Not by killing does one
become noble. By non-killing one becomes noble.

Dhammapada 103 and 270

Buddha never forbids those outside the Buddhist fold from killing, but for the sangha it is out of the question. For Buddha, the sangha was the assembly of monks and nuns; of course they would not kill. (We will leave aside here the degenerate history of monks who actually *have* done so.) We are not monks and nuns, yet we wish to follow the Buddha Way. What do *we* do?

There may be enemies so desperate that we need to fight or even kill them. We let our governments do this. Buddha never rules this out, but in the long history of Buddhism there are very few examples of legitimate killing. Instead of our enemies, we should conquer ourselves. And if we cannot restore life, who are we to take it? To refrain from killing is a precept for all Buddhists.

What would Buddha do about women's rights?

> *You are a Buddha, made of the same stuff as other men and women but also as all past and future Buddhas. There is simply no support for saying women can't become Buddhas.*

> ### *Bankei, The Hoshinji Sermons*

Despite Buddhism's origins in the sexist culture of ancient India, Buddha always taught that women could become awakened just as well as men. In one well-known Buddhist text, a disciple is changed into a woman. This illustrates that, deep down, nothing is either male or female. Not only are all people equally of the same substance, that substance is the same as the bodies of Buddhas.

Buddha taught women, initiated them into the sangha, and preserved their stories of awakening. Bankei did the same two thousand years later. All this time Buddhism has fought against sexism. That battle continues and has the power of Buddha behind it. If women can become Buddhas, we don't even need to discuss whether they can become priests or presidents.

What would Buddha do about hate crimes?

*If a believer breaks a precept out of craving, I say
it's no crime; but if he breaks a precept out of hatred,
it is a serious offense, a grave fault, a degenerate
act that causes terrible harm to the teaching.*

The Definitive Vinaya Sutra 24

There are three great vices in Buddhism: ignorance, craving and hatred. The first two are natural to us; Buddha does not hold it hard against us if they lead us astray. Hatred is not natural; it is learned, so its presence signals real corruption.

Because only hatred is alien and unnatural to us, only action arising from hatred is truly immoral. We are often amoral when we act from desire or ignorance, but this does not arouse Buddha's condemnation. Hateful acts alone warrant adjectives like "grave" and "degenerate." Not only do such acts cause harm (ignorant acts do this as well), they cause it willfully, often for the sake of the harm itself. This destroys people and darkens our view of the truth. Buddha was a tolerant and easy leader and most Buddhist systems of justice have been so as well. Compassion blends with wisdom in judgment. But when wisdom sees hatred, justice grows stricter.

What would Buddha do to help a young person who has gone astray?

> *The cannibal asked, "How can I abandon the thing that made me give up royalty, endure the wilderness, break the law, and ruin my reputation?"*
>
> *But the bodhisattva answered, "Those are exactly the reasons you should give it up."*

Jatakamala 31.85

Isn't this dialogue both ridiculous and poignant? You have to figure the bodhisattva is going to turn out to be right, but I can really sympathize with the cannibal or the youngster who has gone astray. It's not that these choices tempt me (I love trying new foods, but...)—rather I can deeply understand our feeling of wanting to stick with a strong choice, especially when we've paid a steep price for it. The cannibal has given up everything to be a cannibal; now Buddha asks him to give up even that. It's too much to bear!

In the end, Buddha is right. Not all things are worth the price we pay for them, even when the price is already paid. No matter how strong we grow in carrying our burdens, we are still wise to set some down. In the story, Buddha does change the cannibal's mind and the cannibal is grateful. We too should work to change the minds of those stuck in evil ways.

What would Buddha do in response to something really good?

*Give praise to everyone who tells the truth. Tell them,
"Everything you say is great!" When people do the
right thing, tell them you approve and give them your
encouragement.*

Bodhicharyavatara 5.75

It's about time to talk about something good in this book! Not everything we face in our lives is a problem. So here is a word from Buddha
on praise: go for it!

Buddha trusts you not to praise someone who is acting nice simply to curry favor. But when someone is really doing the right thing,
your words might give them strength to go further on that road. Speaking words of truth is often hard; hearing an affirming echo never hurts.
Who knows? Your voice might strike the first note in a chorus.

(By the way, this is how the modern world moves forward. You
speak first, then the media picks it up. This opens the possibility for
change.)

What would Buddha do when right and wrong aren't clear?

> *Something can seem bad but be good. Just the same, something bad may not look it. Right action is not obvious right off the bat.*

> **Jatakamala 28.40**

Buddha encourages us to act and not delay. But since appearances can be deceiving, even in the realm of right and wrong, this does not mean we should act without thinking.

"Right action" is one of the eight aspects of the Noble Path. We must preserve right action as we walk, no matter how gray or confusing the world makes our path. At times of deception we need to use both our immediate moral sense and our careful, reasoned intelligence to keep us going in the right direction. No, this is not easy. Who ever told you it was easy? Buddha said we can do it, though, and so we can.

Walking the Walk on the Noble Path

This section and the next one range over a whole world of territory. All this territory is contiguous because it extends from one central question: How do I walk the Buddha walk when I face practical, worldly dilemmas? In this section I've collected problems each of us must solve as individuals on our own. The answers help us summon the moral action and beneficial conduct we need in the face of a world that tempts us to serve ourselves only.

On such subjects, Buddha said less than we might today want. If he were alive now, his followers—to say nothing of the media hordes who would ceaselessly hound him—would ask pointed questions and demand pragmatic answers. That is our way. Although Buddha lived so long ago, a surprising number of the answers in this section come from the early years of the tradition. This continued liveliness testifies to the refreshingly down-to-earth character of Buddha's teachings. His voice echoes in contemporary problems as well as among contemporary teachers. His wisdom can still make the Noble Path seem as familiar as Main Street.

What would Buddha do when he can't find the time to learn?

Good speech has understanding as its essence. Learning has concentration as its essence. The wisdom and learning of one who is hasty and negligent do not increase.

Sutta Nipata 329

Buddha could not be clearer: if you try to learn too fast, you make mistakes. This is true for everyone, since life is like a vast school from which we never want to graduate. We're here learning, everyday—or we *should* be.

Buddha's words come to life in my teaching. I strive to convince my students (blissfully ignorant of English style) and my colleagues (willfully ignorant of English style) that good speech and writing depend on understanding. The writer must understand what she means to say, and write so the reader can understand it. In this lies learning, and, as Buddha says, it takes concentration. Not only that, it takes time. We cannot be hasty or negligent or we will stop learning in the school of life. Even Buddha took years to learn everything his gurus taught. It will take us longer.

What would Buddha do to find his fortune?

> *Service to parents, support of spouse and children,*
> *and honest work—this is the greatest fortune.*

> ### *Sutta Nipata 262*

Buddha is saying a great deal here. First, he is telling us of our duties, the same responsibilities people have had since the beginnings of culture. He mentions our parents, the previous generation; our spouses, this generation; and our children, the next generation. We owe them service and support, with all that entails. In this way we root ourselves in history and extend our family into the future. The other responsibility Buddha mentions is work—simple or arcane, menial or rarified, it must be honest. Through the honesty of work we guide our society into the future.

I have spoken of responsibilities, but Buddha spoke of our "greatest fortune." The very burdens of adulthood become, when we act from our Buddha nature, our reward and our joy. So the wise have counseled us, from Ecclesiastes ("Enjoy life with the wife whom you love...because that is your reward in life and in your toil") to Freud (the point of life is "love and work"). Service, support, work—these are our blessings.

What would Buddha do in the heat of an argument?

[Right speech] is well-said, not ill-said; sense, not nonsense; pleasing, not displeasing; true, not untrue.

Sutta Nipata 449

We all need to speak out. Sometimes we even do it wisely and well, but usually we do it in the grip of anger, frustration or ignorance. I cannot tell you how many times I've felt anger impelling me toward some cutting comment to my wife, known how foolish it would be to give in to this anger, and done it anyway, just for the twisted pleasure of it. We are all like this.

Buddha suggests another way. Monks are never to engage in such destructive speech; for them it is a rule to obey. For us it is a precept to follow, but it is a good one. Think back on your life and count the times you have changed someone or something for the better through insults and falsehoods. I personally can't think of even one. But I have changed persons and things for the better, even in the midst of fights, by following Buddha's advice. Sometimes, when my wife and I can hold our tongues until our speech is pleasing, our fights turn to work and our work to joy.

What would Buddha do about protecting endangered species?

> *Just as a mother would protect her own child, her only child, with her life, so should one cultivate an unbounded mind toward all beings.*

> **Sutta Nipata 149**

A mother knows her own life cannot be separated from her child's. We *are* our relationships, so who are we apart from our children? A mother's mind and a child's mind have no boundaries; they include each other. This is why she defends her child as she would her own life. In defending her child she *is* defending her own life.

As with a mother and child, so with us and our world. Our lives here are inconceivable without the whole of the biosphere surrounding us. Our minds should embrace all beings as inseparable from ourselves. With our great power we are the mothers of all the beings of the world. We must protect each of them; an endangered species is like a gravely ill child. What mother could turn her back?

What would Buddha do about a competitive co-worker?

Only when faced with the activity of enemies can you learn real inner strength. From this viewpoint, even enemies are teachers of inner strength, courage, and determination.

The Dalai Lama

Even if you are a person who feels friendly with everyone, you still face competition everyday. In a sense, your competitors are your enemies. But in a larger sense, your enemies are your teachers, as the Dalai Lama says.

We love our friends and they wish us well, but they don't often test us or push our boundaries as persons. It is precisely those people who do *not* wish us well that force us to summon up our strength, courage and determination. In this way they become our teachers, worthy of profound gratitude.

When faced with enemies, remember they are offering you a gift your loved ones seldom match. Summon your reserves and honor their gift by defeating them with grace.

What would Buddha do to win over an audience?

> *The teaching of Buddha*
> *is like a great cloud*
> *which with a single kind of rain*
> *waters all human flowers*
> *so that each can its bear fruit.*

Lotus Sutra 5

Buddha knew that every person is like a flower, having its particular needs and yielding a unique fruit. Yet he describes his teaching as being like one rain that nourishes all flowers alike. Buddha's teaching can be of a single kind because each person has the capacity to absorb just the right part to come to fruition. The truth is one, but the flowers and fruits are many.

Whatever we have to impart, we should teach it in this way. We must not distort the message by telling one thing to one person, another thing to another. Though this is tempting, in the long run it divides us from people and them from each other. Instead we must simply state our case (and state our case simply) and allow people to accept it in their own ways. Then, as Jesus said, "By their fruits you will know them" (Matthew 7:20). When we just tell it like it is, it will bear good fruit in all people, though we might have to wait awhile.

What would Buddha do when things are going great?

> *There are four kinds of bliss appropriate for someone enjoying the pleasures of the senses.... The bliss of wealth, the bliss of spending money, the bliss of debtlessness, the bliss of blamelessness.*
>
> **Anguttara Nikaya 4.62**

When you have earned your wealth through honest work, Buddha says enjoy it. When you spend that money on worthy things, that's fine. When you are free of debt, Buddha says congratulations. And when you are free of blame and guilt, Buddha blesses you.

Many people misunderstand Buddha on this point. They think he doesn't want you to have any fun. Absurd! Buddha wants you to enjoy yourself. It's just that he wants you to remember we are all in this together, and if you think only of your own selfish pleasure, you will have no real bliss in the end. So Buddha says make your money through doing good work for others. Spend that money on non-harmful products and experiences. Stay out of the debt that harms you and the economy. And try to do good and not hurt others. If you can do that, go have a blast—you deserve it!

What would Buddha do if he went broke?

> *The thought occurs to him, "Even though my money*
> *is gone, I have received the five benefits it can give,"*
> *and so he feels no despair.*

> **Anguttara Nikaya 5.41**

I am not one of those serene souls who can seemingly live on windfalls and moonbeams. I need money to support my lifestyle. This follows from choices I have made, worldly choices. Nevertheless, though my life is not pure, it can still be good and noble. You are probably similar. We value the spiritual, but we still love this world and the pleasures money can buy in it.

Buddha respects these choices, as long as we can cope when things go awry. He knows this is likely to happen. To prepare us for such a moment, he advises us to remember money's real role. We should not think of money as an end in itself; this will surely lead to grasping and clinging. We should think of it as a means. If we can think of money in this way, we may still enjoy having it but will be ready to live without it. Money gives "five benefits": pleasures for dependents, pleasures for friends, protection from disasters, and the ability to give to both worldly and spiritual causes. Enjoy these benefits while you have money, and when it's gone, be reassured that the money has done its job.

What would Buddha do about giving to charity?

> *Charity is fruitful only when we feel the three pure feelings: feeling joy before the gift is given, giving gracefully, and having pleasure of it after; that is perfect charity.*

Jatakas 390

Buddha was a pragmatist in some ways. He did not think in black and white; he considered the complexity of cause and effect in this mingled world. You might think he would ask us to give as much as possible to charity. Why not give everything and become a monk! He knew why not: because not everyone is ready to be a monk. Not everyone is even prepared to give to charity. When we are not ready to contribute, it is better not to force things. If we do we will come to resent it and create suffering for ourselves and those around us.

The ease of giving is what Buddha promotes here. We need to feel the joy of our charity. Charity, after all, means love as well as generosity; in Buddha's teaching it is inseparable from compassion. We will find this joy in the contemplation, act and memory of giving. Look for the joy—though this might take effort and insight—and give with a glad heart. Then our charity will indeed be perfect.

What would Buddha do about gun control?

*Men who make weapons get no merit from it even
though they make them for protection.*

**Chandrakirti's commentary
on the Chatuhshataka 4.11**

I can imagine Buddha's response when presented with the arguments
of the pro-gun lobby. His reaction is easy to imagine because so many
contemporary Buddhists embody it, whether in protesting the war in
Vietnam or the occupation of Tibet or the grotesque arsenal filling the
world. Buddha would call on us to halt the manufacture, purchase and
use of guns. There are no two ways about it.

The text above points to the truth about weapons. Even though they
may at times be used to protect society, guns ultimately do not help
society, they merely kill living things. There is no merit in this even if society is aided. Why? Because there are other means to protect society
without shedding blood and causing pain. There is always another way.
And what is true for the makers of weapons is even truer for their users.

What would Buddha do to change the world?

> *Smoothing out the earth with leather sheets*
> *Cannot be done for lack of so much hide.*
> *Just put a bit of leather on your feet;*
> *It's like you've covered the entire world!*

Bodhicharyavatara 5.13

Upholstering the world! I love the humor of this answer. Shantideva sees our all too human ways with Buddha's eyes. He knows we have this human tendency to want to change the world—at the greatest cost and effort—before even considering changing ourselves. He doesn't berate us, though; he cheers us on to do the right thing.

When we want to make our lives easier, we have a choice like the one in this stanza. We can change the world (heaven knows it needs it). Or we can change perspective, and maybe transform ourselves (heaven knows we need it!). Is your life hard because you need a bigger place or because you have too much junk? Are things difficult because your job doesn't pay enough or because you spend too much? Is life frustrating because you have no lover or because you feel you need one? Think carefully before you decide. Then change what needs changing.

What would Buddha do about preserving the environment?

When you throw away your spit and toothbrushes, you must hide them well away from sight. Dumping waste in places that we share and in the water system leads to ill.

Bodhicharyavatara 5.91

Buddha (and Shantideva) lived long before we humans had the power to deeply damage the world. Yet they saw what even simple societies could do if they didn't care for the world around them. If even by dumping human waste we foul the earth, I fear the ills we now cause by dumping inhuman waste.

Is there one central message to all Buddhist teaching? If so, it is that everything interrelates, it all rises and falls in interdependence. We have all heard the terms "sustainable" and "unsustainable" regarding our mining, foresting, fishing, farming. If, as Buddha says, it all rises and falls together, then what do you suppose "unsustainable" means? Think about that while you're filling another plastic bag.

What would Buddha do in picking a partner?

If on the path you don't meet your equal, it's best to travel alone. There's no fellowship with fools.

Dhammapada 61

People today suffer from the twin evils of arrogance and false egalitarianism. We think we're great, but we don't want to judge others. We find it hard to proclaim: "That guy is a loser," or "He's too slick." We can't manage to simply say, "He's not smart enough to be with," or "He's not moral enough to hang around." I find this chilling, even while it is my own problem.

Buddha does not have this problem; he says make a judgment and move on. Buddha does not pretend things are any different than they are. Hang with dumb people and you get dumber. Hang with sleazy people and you get sleazier. Make your choices and accept responsibility for them. But remember: if you choose those unworthy of you, you will never experience real fellowship, never have a partner.

What would Buddha do when forced into a fight?

*Somehow I draw my enemies to me: They harm me,
but my karma brings them here. And so they go to hell
because of me. I'm the one who sends them to their
doom.*

Bodhicharyavatara 6.47

No question, finding compassion for our enemies is hugely difficult. It takes at least a lifetime of practice to approach this goal. Shantideva's words help me because they highlight the deep irony of harm: we are our enemies' enemy.

We think of enemies as those who harm us in the here-and-now. This perspective is too narrow. Buddha does not primarily value things that make our separate selves happy. He also does not envision this single life as the only one we have. Whether or not we believe other lives will follow, we can see that people who try to harm us are already harming themselves by hurting their ability to love and cheapening their own lives. We should also realize that, even willy-nilly, we brought this situation on. We are the cause of *their* harm. We are all in this together. The only escape is compassion. Thinking this way clarifies why we need to act with kindness toward our enemies—especially our enemies.

The Buddha
in the Machine

Here we move from the personal practicalities of the world into the realm of institutions. We are all so immersed in institutions we may find it difficult to see where they end and we begin. Still, we come first, even if we forget. These questions and answers should help each of us examine our dealings with the power structures around us.

I adapted the title for this section from the notion of "the ghost in the machine": our human spirit inside our bodies and inside a mechanical society. Think of that spirit as your inner Buddha and the machine as the institutions that enmesh you. Sometimes that machine runs smoothly and we can ride it. Other times, as free speech advocate Mario Savio said, "The operation of the machine becomes so odious, makes you so sick at heart, that you can't take part, and you've got to put your bodies upon the gears and upon the wheels, upon the levers, upon all the apparatus and you've got to make it stop." The machine always starts again, but when we stop it even for a moment, we change it. I hope this section of the book helps you see when to change yourself and when to change the machine. These are our social responsibilities, as sacred as anything under heaven.

What would Buddha do about
noisy neighbors?

The sound of the valley stream is His long, broad tongue;
The form of the mountains, that's His pure body.
During the night I heard a thousand verses chanted;
Now how can I impart them to others?

Su T'ung-po

We all know the tremendous resentment that wells up when someone nearby is making too much noise. I myself am irrationally incensed by the barking of my neighbor's dog. But is the barking or the nearby party or the leaf-blower down the street intrinsically making a bad sound? The party may be the loudest and latest of these; perhaps it seems worst. But party sounds resonate with life and joy. There is nothing wrong with these sounds.

The perception of sounds happens in our minds. The resentment of sounds happens in our minds. It is entirely up to us how to perceive such things. For the poet, Su T'ung-po, all sounds were the Buddha's voice. Now that's the way to be. We need to emulate Su. If he can do it, we can do it, or at least we can die trying. Face it: It's easier than getting that dog to shut up.

What would Buddha do about making money?

With a mind of trust and harmony he conducted all kinds of business, yet he did not find his pleasure in the profit it made him.

Vimalakirti Sutra 2

We think of Buddha himself as purely spiritual, removed from the hustle of the marketplace (or "The Market," as we now grandly call it). But he knew not all his followers could be so pure; we would want to make money. Though monks are forbidden to handle money, the rest of us have got to pay the bills. But accumulating cash should not replace other values.

This passage gives us two basic principles for doing business wisely. First, we need to maintain our Buddha mind as we work, even in the sorts of businesses where duplicity usually rules. With minds of trust and harmony, we can build personally gratifying business relationships. Second, no matter what harvest we reap, we need to find our pleasure in deeper things than profit. Profit is fine; making it our goal is harmful. This is where financier Ivan Boesky falls short of Buddha wisdom: profit is good, greed is not. One of the great trials we face in business is retaining that distinction.

What would Buddha do as a boss?

A good employer ministers to her servants and employees in five ways: by assigning them work they can manage; by giving them food and money; by supporting them in sickness; by sharing special delicacies; and by granting them leave when appropriate.

Digha Nikaya 31

Naturally the role of a boss has changed in 2500 years. Perhaps we no longer expect bosses to provide food for their employees. But Silicon Valley managers have found that the more food they provide, the more work gets done. Perhaps Buddha's saying is not so dated.

Look at Buddha's other words. An employer should assign work according to employee strengths. This is just what modern-day management gurus teach. She should give them money, of course, but also support them in sickness. What is this but healthcare benefits? As for "sharing special delicacies," what is this but profit-sharing? And how about "granting them leave." Think of the recent fights over maternity leave. The benefits we have fought so hard for (still are fighting for!) have been the wisdom of Buddha for millennia.

What would Buddha do at a boring job?

Look for sand when you're checking the rice.
Look for rice when you're tossing the sand.

Dogen, "Instructions for the Cook," Shobogenzo

We are easily lulled into dullness. Our minds are so keen that if we don't occupy them, they go to sleep, even when we are still awake. Most people's work days are like this. If we succumb to this, we miss out on so much!

Dogen's words to the cook bring us back to our task right now. Even the most menial job comes alive when we look into it. This is hard to believe, but I have found it true in my own work. Making the coffee impeccably requires real attention. Then serving that coffee gives real satisfaction. Think of meditation: nothing could be more bland, yet when we do it right it is never boring. When we're checking the rice we have to look closely. When we're throwing out the sand we must be careful. Through this attention we find satisfaction; those grains of rice become little treasures.

What would Buddha do when stuck waiting for a flight?

Some have encountered intolerable suffering. They have spent up to twenty years in prison, and yet some of them have told me that it was the best time of their lives, because they were able to do intense prayer, meditation, and virtuous practice.

The Dalai Lama

The Dalai Lama has lived decades in exile, compassionately battling for the freedom of Tibet and his many followers in prison there. His commitment to nonviolence is well-known—he has received the Nobel Peace Prize. But here is a lesser-known kind of nonviolence: nonviolence when we're frustrated. We tend to get angry when we're trapped; the Dalai Lama suggests we use it as an opportunity.

He shows how we can practice virtue anywhere, even in prison. Most people succumb to violent bitterness and anger there, but some see the extraordinary opportunity it affords. In fact the Dalai Lama sometimes seems to wish for the freedom of prison, the liberation of time. In our busy lives, like him we wish for just such freedom, but it comes at too high a cost. Instead, why don't we try to practice reflection, or meditation, or prayer when we we're trapped somewhere. It's not a crime. If people can find freedom even in prison, surely we can find it sitting in the terminal.

What would Buddha do about trusting the media?

One's ears hear a lot; one's eyes see a lot. The wise person should not believe everything seen or heard.

Undanavarga 22.17

How much we see and hear! We are bombarded with information. Not for nothing is this called the "Information Age." Unavoidably, this so-called "information" lacks substance and contains bias. This holds true even for what we call "the news."

Whether we get our news from newspapers, television, the internet, inside sources or scholarly studies, we must question it. Buddha tells us the wise person should not believe everything. Well then, how do we decide what to believe? We look into the intention of the source. Intention matters profoundly to Buddha; he taught that our intentions are sometimes more important than our actions. Apply this to the media. The action may be a "news program," but what is the intention? Question that and you will begin to see through the surface and perceive the complexity of things.

What would Buddha do about New Age gurus?

Psychic powers and wonders are not to be revealed.
Anyone who reveals such powers openly is doing wrong.

Vinaya Cullavagga 5.8.2

Many gurus in the West try to prove their status by demonstrating psychic powers. Such powers are truly impressive, so if they convince others that they have these abilities, people follow them as teachers. But having those powers is no guarantee of possessing wisdom. This is why Buddha told his followers not to display such powers. Wisdom, not psychic power, is the mark of a good teacher.

There is another reason Buddha warned us against psychic powers. He believed they exist, but they don't help us. Such powers are like drugs; they are distractions that lead people away from what really matters in life: love and wisdom. Whether we think we have psychic abilities or our teacher possesses them, we are better off turning away from that playground and paying attention to living a wise and loving life. To do that we need to concentrate on using our normal powers—and lots of them.

What would Buddha do if he was a crime victim?

Whoever harms an innocent man, pure and faultless, his evil comes back at him like dust thrown into the wind.

Sutta Nipata 662

What would Buddha do when unfairly injured? He would know he didn't have to do anything. He would simply let things take care of themselves. The evil action of injuring an innocent person leads to an evil consequence later. This is the way of the world. Sometimes the harm comes back obviously and immediately, like dust blown back in the thrower's face. Sometimes the harm is returned slowly and subtly, as in the fall of an empire. Standing firm in one's innocence may require real patience, but it is true wisdom.

Buddha called this principle karma, the law of cause and effect. Because karma is inexorable, Buddha knew that the innocent person did not need to punish the guilty. They punish themselves. All things must pass, even the power of injustice. This may take a long time (think of Nelson Mandela, the South African leader imprisoned for 27 years), but things will come around in the end (think of Nelson Mandela, beloved president of his reborn country).

What would Buddha do when sickened by politics?

> *We say "Dirty Politics," but this is not right. Politics is necessary as an instrument to solve human problems, the problems of human society. It itself is not bad; it is necessary.*
>
> ### The Dalai Lama

From time to time I am tempted to stop voting, signing petitions or writing letters to Congress. I get so discouraged with the pettiness and corruption of politics that I doubt it can accomplish what it must. Most of us go through these phases (which sometimes never end).

We may be right to be sickened, but we are not right to stop acting. Buddha's wisdom reminds us that motivation makes the deed good or bad. Even in the backrooms of Washington or London or Moscow, people are practicing the art of the possible. If their intentions are clean, their work is too. We should honor them in what must at times be a terrible job.

By the way, I suggest we honor them best by being their consciences. If they make us sick, we must make them well.

What would Buddha do about capital punishment?

It is great compassion which we call the Buddha Mind.

Amitayur Dhyana Sutra 17

Buddha's entire teaching stands opposed to capital punishment. I could have picked a dozen other quotes to place here, some more specific than this one. I chose the one above because it goes beyond the specific question and teaches us a universal lesson.

Killing, even killing animals, causes pain. All living things want to keep living. So what about a person who has shown no regard for others, who kills with evil intent? Does such a person deserve to live? Buddha might admit such a person really doesn't deserve to live, but he would add more. We do not have the ability to be just in matters of death and life. We cannot dispense life, so how can we dispense death? Further, in such matters of punishment we do not always know what is wise, but we do know what is compassionate. Let us be strong and act on what we know. When we do this our mind will be the Buddha Mind.

What would Buddha do about patriotism?

> *Every country has faults. In one it's too cold, in another too hot, or there's famine, or sickness, or crime, or the government is corrupt. The practitioner should not be attached to any of these countries and their various evils.*
>
> ### Tso-ch'an San-mei Ching

No country is perfect and we know it. Yet the dream of patriotism is so hard for us to relinquish. Even atheists excuse their nation's failures and march off to fight its wars for slavery or oil or whatever economic need rules the day.

Buddha is not interested in countries; we shouldn't be either. In his time, government had a fairly weak influence over people. It wasn't central to what mattered in life. In our time, countries have powerful influence over people; but other factors, chiefly economic ones, have power over countries. Countries still are not central to what matters in life. Defending a country from evil forces might be worth doing, but defending his country's power over others is simply not something Buddha would do.

What would Buddha do when his country goes to war?

We disrespect people sacrificing their possessions for liquor and such. I ask why we respect them for sacrificing themselves in war.

> **Chandrakirti's commentary**
> **on the Chatuhshataka 4.17**

Chandrakirti asks a powerful question: How is giving one's life to a war any different from giving it to an addiction? Maybe it isn't. An addiction to alcohol forces the alcoholic to choose the high over love, status, health, even life itself. A war forces the soldier (and often the civilian as well) to choose battle over love, status, health, even life itself. It's a bad bargain.

You may object that battle leads to something beyond itself, something greater. Buddha would question both war's means and its ends. What worthy ends are not better achieved through love than through hate? As for sacrificing yourself without killing and for a worthy cause, this is a different matter. Give yourself to saving all living things, by any means necessary. All the Buddhas and bodhisattvas embody this. We should too, but this is not about our countries and not done with violence.

The Big Questions

This final section is for the philosopher in us. We all ponder the "big questions" from time to time, and sometimes they turn very intimate and powerful. Buddhism has an ambiguous history in these matters. The historical Buddha put such questions to the side, saying they did not lead to liberation from suffering. He wanted to bring people back to the present moment. But what if this moment demands tackling those big questions?

When a question like, "Who is it that is asking this question?" hits you hard, it can knock you right over with its power. For me, imagining my death, the end of my own consciousness, can strike with such force that I get physically weak and dizzy (not to mention depressed). At such moments, the big questions become vital, and that makes them crucial to Buddhism as well. In Zen Buddhism these questions are called "the Great Matter of life and death," and answered in brusque and earthy tones. Buddhism gives answers that may be brilliantly philosophical, deeply compassionate, even pretty darn funny. In this category, I ask big questions and hope some of them really hit you. Find one and really let it penetrate you. If it knocks you down, maybe you'll be open to Buddha's picking you back up in a new place. My great good hopes go with you.

What would Buddha do about attending church?

> *For the pure, it is always a holy night. For the pure, every day is the Sabbath. For the pure, with their pure acts, it is always time for worship.*

> **Udanavarga 16.15**

Here Buddha tells us what a real religious ceremony is: the acts of a pure person. This means that worship can happen at all times. In fact, it is always time for worship. Look at the clock! This very moment is the sacred moment. Buddha calls us to give thanks.

Can we go to ceremonies of religions that are not our own? Of course we can. If we keep a pure mind, we will see the beauty and holiness of any religious ceremony we attend, and the worshippers there will be glad we came. If it is always time for worship, we should say yes when asked to.

What would Buddha do about death?

> *Everything together falls apart.*
> *Everything rising up collapses.*
> *Every meeting ends in parting.*
> *Every life ends in death.*

Udanavarga 1.22

Definitive words here from Buddha. Ourselves, the world, indeed all the incomprehensibly great cosmos, will be destroyed and pass away like everything else before it. Such is the way of all things; they come together and they fall apart, regardless of our feelings.

What can we do about this? Nothing, not one damn thing. Should this matter to us? Not at all, not one bit. When the great earth vanishes into air, our little lives will have long been rounded with a sleep. Everything passes away; this is right and fitting for things. To strive against this is vain; instead, we must accept our part in the flow, the unceasing changes that are life. For those already mourning the distant death of the world, I'll let you in on a secret: Buddha teaches that the whole boiling begins again.

What would Buddha do to learn the secrets of the universe?

> *Many statements I have left unsaid. Why have I left them unsaid? Because they are not helpful. They are not fundamental to the holy life. They do not lead to peace, knowledge, awakening, nirvana.*

> *Majjhima Nikaya 63*

The simple answer to this question is that Buddha would not try to learn the secrets of the universe. He didn't teach them, either. In fact, when Buddha was teaching, several students implored him to reveal those secrets and he never did. They asked if the universe is eternal, if the soul and body are the same, if the Buddha continues to exist after death, etc. He never even said whether he knew the answers. Why didn't he speak? Because they just don't matter on the path of awakening.

Buddha taught the path to peace, the path he calls the holy life in the passage above. This path makes us happy, loving and wise. That was what he cared about, and that is what Buddha tells us we should care about. When we get all hot and bothered about questions we can never answer, it is good to remember Buddha's example: he didn't bother himself about such things and he turned out okay.

What would Buddha do about religion?

He becomes a monk in all the different religions of the world so that he might free others from delusion and save them from falling into false views.

Vimalakirti Sutra 8

Extraordinary! Buddha tells us here that the great and wise person, the bodhisattva, does not have to be Buddhist. In fact, this wise person actually enters deeply into other religions, devoting her life to helping others through the means of those religions.

This, I confess, is one of my personal joys in Buddhist doctrine: the fact that the doctrine in the end is not all that important. What matters is following the path of being who we are. If we truly can do this, we can do it within the realm of Buddhism, Christianity, Islam, Hinduism, Atheism, Judaism, Shinto, Confucianism, Animism, Sikhism—the list goes on. What matters is being compassionate and not clinging to the idea that we alone know the truth.

Can we be bodhisattvas and remain committed to other religions? In answer, let me ask another question: Do you think Mother Teresa was lacking something? You don't do you? Neither does Buddha.

What would Buddha do when his prayers go unanswered?

If nothing helps, do not fall into error, thinking, the Buddhas have no blessings; their teaching is false! Think instead, I will feel better when I exhaust my evil karma!

Dakini Teachings 2

Of all forms of Buddhism, the Tibetan school most wholeheartedly embraces prayer and the power of Buddha to help us. But even that tradition, from which these words come, knows magic doesn't always work. Does this mean the tradition is wrong and powerless? Of course not.

We have some free will and there may be other powers who can help us in this life, but we are also strictly bound by our past. Whether we believe, with Buddhists, in karma; or, with Solomon, in casting our bread upon the waters; or, with Freud, that the child is father to the man, we believe in the power of the past. We will see times when nothing we can do now can hold back that power to do us ill. At those times we must remain aware of the past and patient in the present. In this way we will eventually free ourselves.

What would Buddha do when he's hungry?

A monk then asked, "Can you say something that transcends the Buddhas and Ancestors?"

The Master said, "Sesame flatbread."

Blue Cliff Record 77

Perhaps this doesn't sound like a "Big Question" to you. But Zen Master Yunmen here voices the profound wisdom of Buddha, a wisdom that reaches deep down into...the belly. Yes, when it's time for lunch, what could be more important than food? What on earth is the matter with you? Go eat!

The previous paragraph might seem simple, but a thousand years of Zen masters have knocked this "simple" truth against their students' heads—and every once in a while, opened their minds. Buddha teaches being here in the moment. A famous Zen koan says the greatest miracle is sleeping when you're tired and eating when you're hungry. At lunchtime that means feeling hunger and eating food. This is why tasty, fresh-baked flatbread transcends all the celestial Buddhas and the venerated Ancestors of the past. You can *eat* flatbread. Are you hungry?

What would Buddha do to search for perfect knowledge?

Your mind becomes Buddha. Your mind is Buddha. All the Buddhas' ocean of perfect knowledge begins in your very mind and thought.

Amitayur Dhyana Sutra 17

Buddha doesn't have to do anything to gain perfect knowledge. He knows he has it already. He knows *we* have it already. But somehow we seem to be left out of the loop. How ironic that we don't know we have perfect knowledge! What went wrong?

Buddha's words here teach us where to find that perfect knowledge we crave. In this way they help us answer what went wrong with us. The great ocean of Buddha knowledge begins—has always begun—in your mind at this very moment. That ocean of truth is something we gain by looking inside, not outside. As our thought becomes freed from our ego, our mind becomes Buddha; this is the birth of perfect knowledge. We have lost touch with that boundless, oceanic mind, but it remains inside us. When we find the courage to stop clinging to the self, we will find ourselves swimming in that ocean.

What would Buddha do to rejuvenate his spirit?

> *Though you say "He has retreated from the world at the wrong time," life is so very fragile there is no wrong time for religious retreat.*

Buddhacarita 6.21

We feel that life stretches out before us without end. Especially as children we seem immortal. We can play in the world without care for an ending. But we know, deep down, that life is as fragile as a bubble, and as fleeting.

Like a bubble, life is a circle, and though this is the strongest shape on earth, it will pop. Also like a bubble, life is rich with all the colors of the rainbow. We love to immerse ourselves in the colors; we grow drunk on them. Buddha reminds us to be sober. This sobriety awakens the need for retreat. It also is the reason retreat should not be put off: our moments of sobriety cannot be predicted. When they come, we need to take advantage of them in retreat and reflection.

At the time of Buddha, regular people could completely withdraw from the world to follow the religious life. Most of us don't have that option; we must withdraw without withdrawing, looking at the bubble and yet remaining in it. We do not have an easy time. Still, Buddha encourages us to keep our priorities straight.

What would Buddha do for people who are suffering?

In order to save living beings,
They volunteer to descend into
All the hells that are attached
To all the infinite worlds.

Vimalakirti Sutra 8

Who are those people who descend even into hell to help others? These are the bodhisattvas, the wise ones. Who are the bodhisattvas? They are any one of us who act for the good of all. Does this sound like a bit too much pressure for you right now? Okay, why not start by descending into the kitchen and making dinner for some suffering person. If it's hot and seems to take an eternity, you'll know you've made a good start.

By the way, there's another text that talks about Buddha smiling radiantly throughout the universe and then creating an image of himself in hell so the poor souls there will be reborn in the realms of humans and gods. Hey, we all do what we can; let's start with the kitchen.

What would Buddha do to be happy?

Seek health, the greatest blessing; follow virtue. Listen to people; read good books and learn. Be truthful; break the chain of sad attachment. These six paths lead to the greatest good.

Jatakas 84

This is a very general question and a very general answer. This is good, because here general means powerful and inclusive. With these words Buddha gives perhaps the simplest yet most practical life advice in the whole Buddhist tradition.

First, take care of your health; from health comes the strength to walk the other five paths. Next, follow virtue—not perfection, not consensus morality, not indulgence, but virtue. Learn, learn from people, books, the internet, wherever. Tell the truth; this is simple. Finally, break the bonds that tie you to your preconceptions, possessions, gripes, even your loved ones. Some of these you may still keep, but don't be bound to them. When you walk these paths, you walk into the realm of happiness: both for yourself and for all living things. (You didn't think Buddha was talking about just *your* greatest good, did you? Blessedly, these goods go together.)

What would Buddha do when doctrine and reason conflict?

We cannot accept a teaching literally simply because it has been taught by the Buddha; we have to examine whether it is contradicted by reason or not. If it does not stand up to reason, we cannot accept it literally.

The Dalai Lama

Perhaps this quote surprises you. But here the Dalai Lama voices a great strength of Buddhism, its use of the mind. From the very first, Buddhism has focused on the mind and our understanding of the world. Because our experience depends so greatly on our understanding, Buddha taught a new way of viewing the self (or its absence) and mental states. This was the core of his teaching and this core exhibits perhaps the greatest logical consistency in any world religion.

Since Buddha taught a core of logical propositions about life, logic, rather than faith, is central to Buddhism. We should have confidence in Buddha's teaching, but not faith. With confidence we examine the teaching with reason. When reason and the teaching conflict, we let go of the teaching, not reason. In this we are on our own. Each person must actively use her own mind as she walks her spiritual path. That path through life is often hard to find. Buddha encourages you: Be fully alive and use your head!

What would Buddha do about modern science?

> *Do not allow skepticism to blind your eyes*
> *to other worlds.*

Jatakamala 29.7

Please don't get him wrong, Buddha actually favors skepticism—when it is healthy. Healthy skepticism tones the mind. What he warns against is reductive science that denies anything our little minds are too small to comprehend.

I am a very skeptical individual. When I went to graduate school I imagined I would learn to see through the illusions of religion. I have seen through some, it is true, but more importantly I have seen through some of my own illusions. The chief of those illusions is that I see through illusions.

I am sorry to belabor you with paradox, but that seems to be the nature of things. So, following Buddha, let us be skeptical but not allow that skepticism to blind us to the glories of worlds we may encounter but not understand. Worlds are great; we are small. If they are greater than we can believe, perhaps it is not their existence we should doubt, but our own.

What would Buddha do when doubting his spiritual path?

> *Whether chanting Buddha's name will gain me rebirth in the Pure Land, or condemn me to hell, I just don't know…. Still, as I'm incapable of any religious practices, there's no doubt hell would be my home.*

> ***Tannisho II***

Here Shinran, the Japanese Pure Land Teacher, expresses his naked doubt. I doubly love this passage. First because he can reveal his confusion, his smallness before the emptiness of space and time. He confesses he doesn't know if his chanting is good or bad for him. This is touching honesty. Second, I love that despite his deep confusion, Shinran knows what to do: keep chanting. Why not? It's not as if he could be doing anything better.

Shinran has faced himself and seen what makes his life work. It is his practice of chanting Buddha's name. He has realized that chanting makes him a better person, perhaps even a Buddha. There is no reason to stop, no matter how confused he is—even when worrying if the practice is actually harmful. Our lives are just like this. We need to keep doing what we can do, practicing what seems to make us better. This is profound and heartening wisdom for slothful and weak people like me. If you can do better, do it! If not, just be humble and do what you can.

What would Buddha do when others attack his beliefs?

If other teachings are beyond us, it doesn't matter how wonderful they are; we can't embody them. But as every Buddha desires to save all living things from rebirth, don't hinder our shallow practice.

Tannisho XII

How is it that people think criticizing someone's meager efforts is at all helpful? Especially in spiritual practice, we should encourage each other. I fear most spiritual criticism comes from arrogance, not compassion. Some think they alone know "the Right Way." Some could be right, but most must be wrong. Instead of criticism, Buddha turns us toward support and approval, even of the weakest efforts—perhaps especially of the weakest efforts.

When people put down your spirituality—and this is sure to happen—gently remind them you are doing what you can. As in this passage, don't fight with them about who is right. Admit your own path is humble (humility is a very high path, even if others don't know it). You might suggest that if the powers of the universe tend toward good, although their path may be better, perhaps that means your own is acceptable. The last step is remembering to keep practicing your path if they respond in anger. Good luck.

What would Buddha do to follow the Buddha?

> *I tell you, there's no Buddha, no Dharma, no practice,*
> *no awakening. But you get all sidetracked trying to find*
> *something. Blind idiots! Would you stick another head*
> *on top of your own? What do you think you're missing?*

> **The Record of Linji 19**

The great master Linji is universally revered among Zen Buddhists. How could this be when he seems to tell us there is no Buddha, no teaching, and no religious practice?

Here is Linji's secret: he has nothing to teach; this itself is his teaching. Trying to understand and follow Buddha is like sticking Buddha's head on top of yours. How could this help you? Instead, Linji tells us we lack nothing. Ah, but to get a hold of that nothing, that is difficult. We must remember that we are already Buddhas ourselves. It's time to act like it.

What would Buddha do to discover what would Buddha do?

> *Do not be led by rumor, or tradition, or hearsay. Do not be led by the authority of religious scripture, nor by simple logic or inference, nor by mere appearance, nor by the pleasure of speculation, nor by vague possibilities, nor by respect for 'Our Teacher'.*

> ### *Anguttara Nikaya III.66*

Buddha does not want you to be led astray by any form of authority—not religious, not logical, not traditional. Here he warns us against every form of authority. Only when you know something through experience can you accept it as true.

Buddha is a teacher, and speaking as a teacher myself, I can tell you never to believe them simply because they got a Ph.D. or founded a religion. Buddha is just a person, after all, and he surely made mistakes, and maybe we've learned a few things over these last couple thousand years to correct those mistakes. Buddha would like that.

So how do we discover what the Buddha would do? None of the partial methods Buddha mentions are enough, but all of them together, when tested by our experience, show us the way. Sure, Buddha gives some answers, but they are not easy answers because they are only real when we find them ourselves. True answers you must find yourself. Now get going!

Suggestions for Further Reading

I hope the handful of books I recommend help bring Buddhism into focus for you personally. Please take these suggestions as mere hints.

For those seeking an introduction to the richness of the whole Buddhist tradition, I recommend *The Vision of Buddhism*, by Roger Corless (New York: Paragon House, 1989). This book refreshingly opens out onto the landscape of Buddhism without dividing it into neat Western areas.

On Theravada Buddhism, and to give a flavor of early Buddhism, I still recommend the classic *What the Buddha Taught*, by the Sri Lankan monk and scholar Walpola Sri Rahula (New York: Grove Press, revised edition, 1974). This work remains clear as a bell and includes some important texts from the Pali canon.

A compassionate introduction to Mahayana Buddhism comes in the form of Taigen Daniel Leighton's *Bodhisattva Archetypes* (New York: Penguin Arkana, 1998). Leighton's book brings the fundamentals of Mahayana to life in traditional religious figures and in figures from our contemporary world. He challenges and helps us all to live as the bodhisattvas we are.

On Tibetan or Vajrayana Buddhism, I recommend just about anything by the Dalai Lama. His voice is humane, open, and yet profoundly steeped in his tradition. Go to the store or library and pick any one that comes alive for you.

For those looking to learn more about Zen I recommend two books. First, the wide-ranging introduction, *Zen: Tradition and Transition*, edited by Kenneth Kraft (New York: Grove Press, 1988). This nicely rounded book covers both history and practice, and includes chapters by both scholars and Zen masters. For more of a practical approach, including instructions on how to actually meditate, I suggest Robert Aitken Roshi's lovely book, *Taking the Path of Zen* (San Francisco: North Point Press, 1982). Here, as in his other luminous books (read them all!), Aitken Roshi writes with elegance, intelligence, and compassion. This is Buddhism for the new millennium.

One last important suggestion: Please try to read some of the sacred texts of Buddhism. They continue to be the root of Buddhist wisdom. Many suttas from the Pali canon are available on the World Wide Web at http://world.std.com/~metta/canon; they even come with helpful introductions. As for Mahayana Sutras, the *Lotus Sutra*, *Vimalakirti Sutra*, and *Heart Sutra* stand out as clear and vivid even for beginners (I recommend Burton Watson's translations of the first two). The compassionate core of Tibetan Buddhism comes through in Shantideva's beautiful *Bodhicharyavatara* and the songs of Milarepa. Finally, I find the taste of Zen in the new reader, *The Roaring Stream*, edited by Nelson Foster and Jack Shoemaker, and in Kazuaki Tanahashi's collections of the writings of Dogen.

Author's Biography

FRANZ METCALF did his masters work at the Graduate Theological Union, and received a doctorate from the University of Chicago with a dissertation on the question, "Why do Americans Practice Zen Buddhism?" He continues to study psychological development and American Buddhism, and is a contributor to *Buddhist Spirituality*, as well as several scholarly journals. He currently works with the Forge Institute for Spirituality and Social Change, serves on the steering committee of the Person, Culture and Religion Group of the American Academy of Religion, and teaches college in Los Angeles. His Buddhist path has not yet gotten him to annutara-samyak-sambodhi, but it has gotten him to the top of Mt. Whitney and he believes if the Buddha had tasted properly aged red varietals, he would never have forbidden alcohol for the sangha.